# JESUS IS VICTOR

# JESUS IS VICTOR

## A. W. Tozer

Compiled and edited by Gerald B. Smith

**Authentic**

This edition first published 2011 by Authentic Media Limited
Presley Way, Crownhill, Milton Keynes, MK8 0ES
www.authenticmedia.co.uk

**British Library Cataloguing in Publication Data**

A catalogue record for this book is available from the British
Library

ISBN-13: 978-1-85078-899-7

Unless otherwise stated, Scripture quotations are from the
Authorised Version of the Bible

Cover design David McNeill
Printed in Great Britain by Cox and Wyman, Reading

# Contents

# Foreword

Aiden Wilson Tozer is remembered by many as an effective preacher of God's written Word. And those who knew him best testify to his consistent practice of the truths he proclaimed. In the years since his death in 1963, there has been in conservative Christianity a growing wave of respect and gratitude for this Spirit-taught prophet.

In Toronto in 1961, Tozer preached a series of messages from the book of Revelation. Unfortunately only 14 tapes, covering the first 10 chapters of Revelation, can be located. That explains why this volume of 12 chapters cannot be considered an exposition of the entire book. Rather, it should be received as a volume of still timely spiritual lessons discovered and preached by Tozer in the mature years of his long public ministry.

Surely it would have been the author's desire that all who pursue the truth in Revelation determine to be among the "overcomers"—resting their faith on the goodness and grace of a loving and just Creator God.

*Gerald B. Smith*
*Fort Myers, Florida*
*1989*

# Introduction

The following paragraphs are the thoughts and words of the author, A.W. Tozer, as he explained to his Toronto congregation his own approach to the Revelation.

The Revelation is a great book because it is the revelation of Jesus Christ! It is not, as some suppose, a book just for theologians, scholars and historians. Although the book presents a complex message, it was written for ordinary people like us.

We have choices as to what we will do with the Revelation. I warn you that it is entirely possible to turn the Revelation into a source of blight to your soul. On the other hand, it is possible to find in this Revelation a great source of light and blessing.

As far as I am concerned, we are dealing in the Revelation with the Word of God. To try to plumb divine mysteries and to learn divine truth without sorrow in our hearts and tears in our eyes is vanity and futility 10 times multiplied.

Revelation raises questions that none of us can answer. There are many details in God's plan for the end of this age that we do not know. Admittedly, some preachers seem able to preach wonderful sermons about things they do not know, but I refuse to be placed in that category.

Here is the method that I must follow as we proceed in our study:

- I will not attempt to interpret or explain all of the symbols and figures of speech as they appear.
- I will not arbitrarily force every passage to fit some prophetic pattern or idea. (If you want to take that route—which, I repeat, I will not take—I warn you that you may do it at the terrible expense of spiritual dishonesty! Or, short of that, you will narrow down your mind to a point where you can never expand or grow—where the Lord can find nothing further to say to you.)
- I will freely admit that there are symbols, personalities and figures that I cannot understand or explain.
- Positively, I will identify the main points to discover the underlying spiritual lessons.
- I will emphasize the great central truth that dominates the Revelation: the truth that when God in heaven gets enough of this world's sin and rejection, violence and rebellion, He will wait no longer. He will do something about it!

We need not decipher and decode mysterious symbols to determine the outcome of this conflict of the ages. There is a plain and radiant theme from the beginning to the end of the Revelation: Jesus is Victor!

That theme will be our theme in these meditations.

*A.W.Tozer*
*Toronto*
*1961*

# 1.

# The Theme of Revelation: "Jesus Is Victor!"

The Revelation of Jesus Christ, which God gave unto him, to shew unto his servants things which must shortly come to pass; and he sent and signified it by his angel unto his servant John: who bare record of the word of God, and of the testimony of Jesus Christ, and of all things that he saw. Blessed is he that readeth, and they that hear the words of this prophecy, and keep those things which are written therein: for the time is at hand . . .

For I testify unto every man that heareth the words of the prophecy of this book, If any man shall add unto these things, God shall add unto him the plagues that are written in this book: And if any man shall take away from the words of the book of this prophecy, God shall take away his part out of the book of life, and out of the holy city, and from the things which are written in this book.

He which testifieth these things saith, Surely I come quickly. Amen. Even so, come, Lord Jesus.

The grace of our Lord Jesus Christ be with you all. Amen.

Revelation 1:1-3; 22:18-21

Have you ever heard of a person eagerly reading an interesting book, then suddenly deciding to abandon it without
reading the last chapter? The last chapter ties together the
threads of the narrative; it summarizes the arguments; it
climaxes the action. You and I would agree that to close a
book without reading the final chapter would be to read
without purpose and without satisfaction.

I have had people tell me that although they read the
Bible, they stop short of Revelation—the final "chapter."
Imagine! That particular Bible book announces itself as
the Revelation of Jesus Christ. It forecasts the consummation of all things and introduces the new order. How
can readers form a balanced understanding of God, sin,
unbelief and divine judgment if they ignore so important a book? In these crisis days of world government,
no Christian can afford to ignore the climactic Revelation.

We may take one of only two stances in regard to this
prophetic "unveiling"—this portraying of the future
return of Jesus Christ to this earth, to this world that
once rejected Him as Messiah and crucified Him at
Calvary. We may ignore it, in effect despising it and jeer-
ing at the prospect of a future divine intervention affecting the entire world. Or we may embrace it, cheering for
the promised victory of a righteous Ruler, the coming
King of kings.

Those who ignore Revelation take their place with the
many who believe a humanistic view of life is sufficient:
that men and women are responsible captains of their
own souls. They take their place with the defiant multitude who shout the age-old refrain: "We will not have
this Man to rule over us!"

Those who take Revelation seriously are convinced of
an actual heavenly realm as real as the world we now
inhabit. They are persuaded that the day of consummation

nears when "the kingdom of the world" becomes "the kingdom of our Lord, and of his Christ," who "shall reign for ever and ever" (Revelation 11:15).

## God is sovereign

Living in this generation, we are fully aware that the competitive world and our selfish society have brought many new fears to the human race. I can empathize with those troubled beings who lie awake at night worrying about the possible destruction of the race through some evil, misguided use of the world's store of nuclear weapons. The tragedy is that they have lost all sense of the sovereignty of God! I, too, would not sleep well if I could not trust moment by moment in God's sovereignty and omnipotence and in His grace, mercy and faithfulness.

The prevailing attitudes of fear, distrust and unrest permeating our world are known to all of us. But in God's plan some of us also know a beautiful opposite: the faith and assurance found in the church of Jesus Christ. God still has a restful "family" in His church. As believers we gladly place our confidence in God's revelation of Himself. Although the material world has never understood our faith, it is well placed in the Scriptures. The Bible tells us many things we could learn in no other way.

This amazing Revelation——the final section of the holy Scriptures—tells us plainly that no human being and no world government or power will have any control or any say in that fiery day of judgment yet to come upon the earth. John's vision of things to come tells us clearly and openly that at the appropriate time the direction and administration of this world will be taken away from men and women and placed in the hands of the only Man who has the wisdom and power to rightly govern. That Man is the eternal Son of God, our Lord Jesus Christ.

Revelation describes the age-ending heavenly and earthly events when our Lord and Savior is universally acknowledged to be King of kings and Lord of lords. All will acclaim Him victor. God's Revelation leaves us with no doubt about that.

In our present period of time, however, there is little recognition of God's sovereignty or of His plan for His redeemed people. Go into the marketplace, into our educational institutions and—yes—even into our popular religious circles, and you will find a growing tendency to make mankind large and to make God small. Human society is now taking it for granted that if God indeed exists, He has become our servant, meekly waiting upon us for our will.

## Believers are the true realists

In the face of this kind of human thinking, I want to make a case for the committed Christians in this world. We are the true realists. We confess that we do not hold the powers of life and death in our own hands. We have sensed the importance of John's vision in the Revelation. We are assured that God is alive and well and that He has never abdicated His throne. While others may wonder and speculate concerning God's place in the universe, we are assured that He has never yielded to any of His creatures His divine rights as Lord of man and nature.

It is for this reason that the Christian believer, related to God by faith, is assured of final victory. Even in the midst of earthly trials, he or she is joyful.

The unbeliever, who boastfully will "take my chances," can only remain cynical. Deep within, he or she discovers doubts and uncertainties multiplying daily. Tell that person about this Revelation, about the certainty of Jesus Christ's ultimate victory, of God's promise of new heavens and a new earth, and he or she can only react with the cynic's biting contempt: "Who cares about fables and empty promises? No person in his right mind would ever confess that he has been reading the book of Revelation!"

Take my word for it. Men and women who think they have all the answers about this life and the next have been mouthing their brave words for generations. They are big, challenging words, but they come from puny, empty hearts and minds. These infidels are too blind to recognize or acknowledge that God does have an eternal plan—a divine plan in which mankind is never permitted to utter the first word or the last.

The fact is that God has always been God—and He always will be God. He knows all about our human beginnings. He has had to consult with no one about anything!

One day that little bundle of delight, so fondly nurtured by parents and family, finds herself in human consciousness and accepts the fact that she is. It is at that point that her volitional life begins. Until that time, she had nothing to say about anything—absolutely nothing.

## God will have the last word

Have you noticed, in the human family, how encouraged we are by the sound of our own voice? Men and women take to strutting and boasting, and in their pride they may declare their independence of God. Little do they realize that God in His divine sovereignty has reserved the right to take up at the last where He began at the first. It can mean only one thing: human beings are in the hands of God finally, whether they will or not.

I declare this truth in all frankness because God's Word, including the book of Revelation, tells us clearly that our man-made civilizations, so called, will not prevail in the coming day of judgment and consummation.

Secular-minded men and women seem annoyed by the premise that the Creator-God has in mind a plan for ending this age in which we live. They do not want to be told that organizations, governments and institutions cannot expect earthly things to continue as they are for ever and ever. Repeatedly and plainly the Bible tells us to expect Jesus, the Christ of God, to return to this earth in power and glory. People who have long joked about the "invisibility" of the kingdom of God will see it established in righteousness and with authority.

Humans try to ignore God, continuing to make their own ambitious, selfish plans. In the years before World War I, Germany's Kaiser Wilhelm, largely blamed for the beginning of that first world conflict, was exceedingly headstrong. At a chapel service attended by the Kaiser, a faithful German minister preached on the coming again of Jesus Christ to establish God's kingdom of righteousness and peace throughout the earth. Wilhelm was greatly offended and spoke to the minister at the close of the service.

"I never want to hear that kind of a sermon again," he warned the preacher. "Such an event is not at all in keeping with the plans we have for the future and the glory of our Fatherland!"

But Kaiser Wilhelm and, a generation later, Adolph Hitler are merely fading memories—illustrations of that vain human propensity to make ourselves big and God small.

There is vastly more in the Revelation than you or I will ever know while we are on this earth. But just God's urging that we be ready for the announced coming events should be sufficient to keep us expectant, interested—and praying!

## The Revelation has to do with relationships

This Revelation of Jesus Christ has to do with His relationship to the Father, to the human race and to the church. It has to do with His relationship to Israel, to the nations, to our enemy the devil and to the coming judgment. Ministers faithful to the Word of God have always said that Christ can be found on every page of the Bible. In the Revelation, we see Him dominating the eternal future. The message of the book is the almost overwhelming portrayal of Christ's victory, bringing about the final destruction of Satan and all of his works.

Part of our Christian restfulness comes from the fact that we are in the hands of a loving God who has already existed throughout all of the tomorrows. Because all time is in God, the flow of time never concerns God. He never has to run in an effort to catch up with the movement of time. The end of time is seen by God just as easily as the beginning of time.

That is why the Bible tells us that God knows the end from the beginning. That is why a godly man like John, caught up in the Spirit of God, could be shown the outline of future events. They were future to him, and they are future to us. That is because we are in the stream of time. They are not future to God because He is not in the stream of time.

The Revelation is the only New Testament book that may be classified as "predictive" in its character and content. (It has been interesting to me to find in the writings of Blaise Pascal, the great 17th-century scientist and religious philosopher, his conclusion that no true prediction of mankind's future can be found anywhere but in the Christian Scriptures.)

About the predictive quality of the Scriptures we ought to be in agreement. If there cannot be any valid foresight, no revelation from God, nothing to warn us or prepare us for tomorrow, this life on earth would have to be considered a gloomy business indeed. Thankfully, we have a definite word, a promise upon which we can lean. Peter, one of God's special spokesmen, expressed it this way:

> We have also a more sure word of prophecy; whereunto ye do well that ye take heed, as unto a light that shineth in a dark place, until the day dawn, and the day star arise in your hearts: Knowing this first, that no prophecy of the scripture is of any private interpretation. For the prophecy came not in old time by the will of man: but holy men of God spake as they were moved by the Holy Ghost (2 Peter 1:19-21).

## We may count on God's illumination

As Christian believers, we are assured that no matter how dark it becomes around us, God will faithfully provide the illumination of His Spirit. The Old Testament offers in the release of Israel from Egyptian bondage a fitting illustration. When God was moving toward the climax of that deliverance, the darkness of night covered Egypt, but, miraculously, there was light in the dwellings of all of the Israelites. So, too, there is light even now for us who are Christian believers concerning our future. God's Word is a light that shines in a dark place until the morning star rises in our hearts.

Note, for your encouragement, that God has done something special in the Revelation that He has done in no other part of the New Testament. He has promised a divine blessing for those who will read it:

> Blessed is he that readeth, and they that hear the words of this prophecy, and keep those things which are written therein: for the time is at hand (Revelation 1:3).

This should be encouragement enough to read and consider what the Revelation has to say. Although it is significantly complex, the book is modest in size. There are but 22 chapters, and none of them can be considered lengthy. A good reader can read through the book in two or three hours.

God's message in Revelation, viewed as a whole, is a prognosis of events affecting the entire created universe—"the things that must shortly be done" (22:6). Those who give themselves to its reading will sense they are on a fast-moving guided tour, discerning a variety of scenes and events in John's panoramic view of the heavens and earth. In quick succession he takes us from the highest heaven to the deepest hell. We hear the trumpets sounding in heaven and see the woes and judgments that follow upon the earth and its seas. Instead of repenting, people harden their hearts against the God who created them and loved them.

## John sees Jesus

John sees his Lord, Jesus Christ, in several different appearances. He is the dazzlingly radiant Son of man with eyes like blazing fire (chapter 1). He is the victorious Lamb standing before the heavenly throne (chapter 5). He is the Conqueror on the white horse riding down the skies to the marriage supper of the Lamb (chapter 19). John also testifies to his vision of the seven-fold Spirit of God before the heavenly throne, whom he sees as seven blazing lamps (4:5).

As we read, we follow the spectacle of the suffering but triumphant church of Jesus Christ (chapters 7, 19) and the divine seal set upon the righteous. John tells us of the Israel of that future day (chapter 7). He was profoundly impressed to see God's record books opened (chapter 20). John saw the "synagogue of Satan" (2:9, 3:9), but before the vision ended, he foresaw the total defeat and chaining of Satan, his every power destroyed, his every license taken away (20:1-3, 7-10).

The Revelation is sobering, for it is a vision of judgment that is coming upon a sinful, selfish, violent world. John sees the Son of man appearing with clouds to "[swing] his sickle on the earth; and the earth was reaped" (14:14-16). John must have been greatly moved as he viewed the new heaven and the new earth God is preparing for His people (21:1-5). He tells us of the river of life that flows forever and, beside it, the tree of life with its leaves for the healing of the nations (22:1-2).

I speak of these things as still future. Many Christians of past centuries insisted that all the events and scenes in the Revelation were already history, that none of the book was predictive. It is a gracious aspect of our evangelical Christian fellowship that we do not make uniformity in prophetic interpretation the test of Christian orthodoxy. As believers we do not sit in judgment of others whose views on these matters are not identical with our own. Determining the actual day and hour of Christ's return to earth is not the occupation God has assigned to us. Our constant readiness to meet Him when He does return should be our most important consideration.

I have been studying these Scriptures for many years. I am prepared to give my answer to an ancient question: "Are all these scenes in the Revelation history?" I can best answer with some questions of my own:

> Has the sun yet turned black like sackcloth? Has the moon yet become blood red? Have the stars yet fallen from the heavens? (Revelation 6:12-13)

> Has there been a time when the sky receded like a scroll being rolled up? Have the mountains and the islands been moved from their places? (6:14)

> When did the earth experience an invasion of locust-like creatures whose sting killed a third of the world's population? (9:1-11)

If the prophesied destroyer has already appeared and the seven angels of judgment have already done their work (chapters 8-9), would we not have known it?

Would there not be some notice in our history books if four specially commissioned angels and 200,000,000 extraterrestrial cavalry had wiped out a third of earth's population? (9:15-19)

When was the abyss—that bottomless pit—opened to allow Satan to come forth again for a short time? (20:7-8)

No, I do not think all these events have taken place. On the other hand, I do believe that the Word of God tells us we stand on the verge of the most dramatic and far-reaching developments since Adam stood up in the garden of Eden and Eve stood by his side. I do not know all the details of the future. But I do know that our Lord is returning to earth. And in that Day of our Lord, the

Holy City will come down out of heaven beautifully dressed as a bride for her husband (21:2).

We have in the Scriptures many appeals to be ready for that day. We are not to live just for now and for this world. We are to live each day with a view of the world above! I am troubled because the church of Jesus Christ today does not seem to know as much about spiritual victory and rejoicing in the Lord as did our forefathers in the Christian faith and fellowship.

Within my own denominational background, I have read much and reflected often on the ministries of A.B. Simpson and the joyful fellowship of those who associated with him in the late years of the 19th century. One of the godly Christian brothers who joined with Dr. Simpson was an officer in the Salvation Army, Russell Kelso Carter. He and those sincere believers were so enthralled with the scriptural promises of Christ's ultimate triumph that Carter was moved to write a gospel song that is still in our hymnal: "Jesus Is Victor!"

Congregations sang that message often in their services of praise, for they believed it was true. Jesus is Victor indeed! Kelso Carter's song depicts clearly and confidently the major themes that prevail throughout the book of Revelation:

> Jesus is victor—His work is complete,
> Crushing all enemies under His feet.
> Jesus is victor; He died not in vain,
> Risen and glorified, Jesus doth reign!
> Jesus is victor—without and within,
> Saving and keeping and cleansing from sin;
> Jesus is victor, O heavenly Dove,
> Come to abide and make perfect in love.
> Jesus is victor—the heavens shall ring,
> Great king of terrors, where is thy sting?

Jesus is victor—we'll shout o'er the grave,
Glory to God, He is mighty to save!

My word to you is this: Do not neglect, do not ignore God's message to our race in this Revelation of Jesus Christ.

# 2.

# The Prophecy in Revelation, "I Am Coming Soon!"

Behold, he cometh with clouds;
and every eye shall see him,
and they also which pierced him:
and all kindreds of the earth shall wail because of him.
Even so, Amen.
I am Alpha and Omega, the beginning and the ending,
saith the Lord, which is, and which was, and which is to
come, the Almighty.

Behold, I come quickly: blessed is he that keepeth the
sayings of the prophecy of this book . . .

And, behold, I come quickly; and my reward is with me,
to give every man according as his work shall be.
I am Alpha and Omega, the beginning and the end, the
first and the last . . .

He which testifieth these things saith, Surely I come
quickly.
Amen. Even so, come, Lord Jesus.

Revelation 1:7-8; 22:7, 12-13, 20

The Book of Revelation provides strong reinforcement to the prophetic declaration of the other Christian Scriptures: Jesus is coming again. The promise that the Creator God has a divine timetable for inaugurating a new order on this earth is not some novel idea advanced by over-zealous handlers of the Scriptures.

In evangelical churches there has always been an expectant hope of Christ's return to earth based on His own stated promises. The record is clear: many times during His earthly ministry, Jesus declared that He would come again to intervene in human history. From the first century of the Christian era to this present time, every generation of believers has expressed its hope for, and expectation of, Christ's return to earth. Wherever sincere Bible students turn in the New Testament, they find continual reminders that an overwhelming "day of the Lord" is coming and that, in fact, it is imminent!

Who can ignore Jesus' own words on the subject?

> And he shall send his angels with a great sound of a trumpet, and they shall gather together his elect from the four winds, from one end of heaven to the other . . .
> But of that day and hour knoweth no man, no, not the angels of heaven, but my Father only (Matthew 24:30, 31, 36).

The apostle Paul had similar words with the same significance for the believers in Thessalonica:

> For yourselves know perfectly that the day of the Lord so cometh as a thief in the night. For when they shall say, Peace and safety; then sudden destruction cometh upon them, as travail upon a woman with child; and they shall not escape. But ye, brethren, are not in darkness, that that day should overtake you as a thief"
>
> (1 Thessalonians 5:2-4).

The apostle Peter wrote the same message of caution
and spiritual preparation to the believers addressed in
his second letter:

> But the day of the Lord will come as a thief in the night;
> in the which the heavens shall pass away with a great
> noise, and the elements shall melt with fervent heat, the
> earth also and the works that are therein shall be burned
> up. Seeing then that all these things shall be dissolved,
> what manner of persons ought ye to be in all holy con-
> versation and godliness, looking for and hasting unto
> the coming of the day of God (2 Peter 3:10-12).

The Revelation ends with this brief message from the
risen and glorified Christ: "I come quickly" (22:20). The
message of the Revelation that Jesus, the Lamb alone
found worthy, is the ultimate victor is closely inter-
twined with the outline of His return to earth as King of
kings and Lord of lords.

## We are responsible

I find myself often thinking about responsibility. It is
sobering for us to realize that each generation of believers has had its own responsibility to be faithful to the
Bible and its teachings. That responsibility includes the
appeal of our Lord Jesus to watch and pray for the day
of His return.

We must admit that many believers throughout the
long centuries did become weary and discouraged. They
concluded that the Lord was indeed delaying His return.
We have had a demonstration of this disinterest in our
own Christian circles. There has been a definite decline
in prophetic preaching and teaching. I am not alone in

relating this decline to the excesses of preachers and teachers who were carried along by the moving tides of history during the first and second World Wars. These teachers produced many exciting sermons and lectures, complete with colorful charts and books. Week after week they fed congregations with minute details of future events. They were dogmatic in insisting that the old Roman Empire was being restored before their eyes. Many of them regarded Mussolini, who had come to complete power in Italy, as the soon-to-be-revealed antichrist described in the Bible.

They built up all of this to an ultimate climax that did not happen according to their predictions. They presumed to know more about the future than Daniel knew. They considered themselves wiser than Isaiah. They held themselves capable of seeing farther into the future than John the revelator. In a sense, many Christians were "burned" by the extreme and forced interpretations of these would-be prophets. Just as a burned child fears the fire, so Christians of that era came to fear any further exposure to prophetic ideas or study.

## Many yearn to be ready

There is no doubt in my mind, however, that millions of Christians in our day yearn within themselves to be ready to see the Lord when He appears. These are the saints of God who have a real understanding that what our Lord Jesus Christ is to us in our personal lives, moment by moment, is more important than merely dwelling always on what He did for us. A great segment of Christian theology emphasizes the utility of the cross on which Jesus died rather than the Person who died on that cross for our sins.

It may surely be observed that most present-day Christians regard redemption as a kind of cut-and-dried commodity—a commodity they may obtain whenever their minds happen to turn to it. Thus, the entire spiritual transaction takes place without emotional content, without spiritual lift and assurance.

So, for many there is no emotional yearning for the return of Jesus. The best hope they know is a kind of intellectual, theological hope. But an intellectual knowledge of what the New Testament teaches about the return of Christ is surely a poor substitute for a love-inflamed desire to look on His face!

Right here, let me tell you that people have different motives for whatever interest they have in the prophetic Scriptures. Some are just curious—humanly curious! They look upon all the minor details of prophecy as the details of an amazing jigsaw puzzle. They will spend much time and effort trying to put the various pieces together, hoping to be the first to arrive at some new prophetic twist or surprising suggestion. But that motive is improper where the promises and claims of our Lord Jesus Christ are concerned. To approach this book of Revelation simply out of curiosity is, in my judgment, close to sacrilege. I liken it to the interest some might have in examining the cerement, or grave cloth, in which the body of our Lord was wrapped for burial, or in chemically analyzing the blood that was shed for us on Calvary's cross.

## Spiritual truth must be obeyed

In the spiritual realm, truth not acted on in obedience becomes darkness. Our hearing the gospel, for example, was not enough. Within our wills we had to act in faith on God's saving truth. Without such action, we would have been worse off for hearing; we would have added to our guilt the sin of refusing to believe and obey God's truth. So in matters of prophecy, shallow-minded, inquisitive men and women should be warned that God will make the light that is in them darkness if they inquire only for the reason of curiosity.

The Word of God is truly the word of God! We must be careful concerning the motivation of our hearts. Let us never be numbered with those who want to sniff curiously at every truth without the least intention of embracing and obeying what God has revealed.

But there is another kind of human curiosity now prevalent among Bible students. It is the idea of "finding the key to the Scriptures." Many are saying, "I want to find the key that will let me understand the Scriptures." I heard a Bible teacher on a radio broadcast promise his listeners that he could give them the key to a proper interpretation and understanding of the Bible. "Of course," he added, "you will have to write me and ask for it."

If we are serious Christian believers, we know that there is no secret, magical key to unlock the meaning of the Scriptures. God did not give us His Word in the form of a series of interlocking puzzle pieces, the solution dependent upon our finding the proper key to allow everything to fall into place.

No, the point cannot even be argued. The Holy Spirit who in the first place inspired the Holy Writings is the only One who can give us inner illumination as we read and study the Bible. But people are human. They insist upon some easier way. "If I can just find the key, I will have the understanding."

It would be tempting, indeed, if we could approach the book of Revelation with so fascinating a prospect.

"Here is the key to Revelation. Whenever you want to enter the wonderful heavenly palace and take in all the scenes, just use this master key!" The faithful preachers and teachers would have a much different task if such a master key were available. They would not have to pray as much. They would not have to study and search as much. They would not have to meditate as much. They would not have to ask God for light and help. They would be able to spend much more of their time out on the lake matching wits with the fish.

## We will not always agree about the details

I have already made it clear that our fellowship as Christian believers does not rest on our ability to agree concerning the interpretation of the prophetic Scriptures. Many of the acclaimed Christian saints of the past believed in the return of Christ to earth, but they did not necessarily adhere to what we now call the "futurist" school of prophetic interpretation. In what I will have to say in this study of the Revelation, you may find yourself in disagreement with me. That is bound to happen as we explore these important issues. But we remain in fellowship despite such differences of opinion.

We do hold a common belief that Jesus is returning to earth, and that when He comes He will bring about the deathless, tearless kingdom He promised. No one knows the day or the hour of His coming. No one knows all the details of His coming or the exact progression of the events that mark His return. What, then, does God expect of us?

He wants us to continue to evidence love for one another, perhaps as we have never done so before. He wants us to worship Him together and to serve Him. He wants us to send this gracious gospel of Jesus Christ to the ends of the earth. All those things we can do even if our views about the rapture of the church, the great tribulation on earth or the details of Christ's return do not exactly coincide. We are blessed indeed if in regard to Christ's return we can say deep within ourselves, "I am ready. I am prepared. I am among those longing to see Him face to face. Even so, come, Lord Jesus!"

That I have said this much about our spiritual freedom and about our fellowship in spite of differing views concerning the details of prophecy would rule me out of some churches. Years ago, during my ministry in Chicago, I was asked to speak to a well-known congregation across town. At the conclusion of my message I expressed the thought that all of us as Christians should live each day as though Christ might return at once, but we should work for our Lord as though He might not return for a thousand years.

I think the elderly layman who was asked to dismiss the meeting with prayer must have heard only my concluding words that we should work as though Christ might not return for a thousand years. In his prayer he told the Lord, in behalf of the congregation, that "we did not get very much out of the sermon." And during the rest of my years in Chicago, I did not receive another invitation to speak in that church! I could only assume that the leaders took it for granted that I was not expecting the return of the Lord for at least another millennium. And that ran counter to their understanding of things.

Actually, my message had centered on our being ready for Christ's return. I consider that the important emphasis. Christ's imminent return should underscore our need to be holy, joyful people, watching for that blessed hope.

As Christian believers who follow the Lamb, we are privileged to know the general outline concerning the end of the age and the arrival of the day of the Lord. The promise is that Christ will appear first to His waiting saints. In a twinkling of an eye, they will be changed, glorified and then caught up to be with Him. In that same instant, all of the righteous dead will be raised from their graves. All will be translated with the Lord Jesus to the wondrous site of the marriage supper of the Lamb.

In the view held by many, this translation of the saints is also the signal for the earth and its inhabitants to be plunged into the baptism of fire and blood known as the great tribulation. The battle of Armageddon will follow, and after that, Christ will return to earth in triumph to reign for a thousand years with His faithful and over-coming bride, the members of His glorified church.

Remember that we are God's believing and expectant people. We are not insects; we are the people of God. In faith we have the right and the privilege to rise from bended knee with faces turned to God, each of us gladly confessing, "I belong to God through Jesus Christ, my Lord. I know that this whole world rightfully belongs to Jesus Christ, who is coming soon!"

## The rightful owner will take over

The crux of the whole matter is this: our wonderful, created world will be restored to its rightful Owner. I for one look forward to that day. I want to live here when Jesus Christ owns and rules the world. Until that hour, there will be conflict, distress and war among the nations. We will hear of suffering and terror and fear and failure. But the God who has promised a better world is the God who cannot lie. He will shake loose Satan's hold on this world and its society and systems. Our heavenly Father will put this world into the hands that were once nailed to a cross for our race of proud and alienated sinners.

It is a fact. Jesus Christ is returning to earth. The Revelation teaches it. Daniel teaches it. Isaiah teaches it. Jeremiah teaches it. Go to the Gospels written by Matthew, Mark, Luke and John. They teach it. Read the promises in the Acts. Read them in Romans and the rest of Paul's epistles. Find the same message in Peter's important two letters to the churches. Jesus Christ is returning to earth!

The Scriptures inform us that Jesus came once to die for our sins. He will come again to claim His redeemed people. He came once to go down under the steamroller at man's feet. He will come again to renovate and restore the earth and to raise the righteous dead from the dust of their graves. I like Isaiah's expression of that coming day of resurrection and glorification:

> Thy dead men shall live,
>> together with my dead body shall they arise.
> Awake and sing,
>> ye that dwell in dust (Isaiah 26:19).

We cannot even imagine the singing for joy and the shouts of victory when Christ comes for His own, when the righteous saints come forth in new and glorified bodies.

Surrounding the conference grounds at Glen Rocks, Ontario, are thousands and thousands of wild canaries —a part of the goldfinch family. They have always intrigued me. As long as they are feeding in large flocks, they are quiet and receive little attention. But stir them up with some kind of activity, and they all begin to sing together even as they fly away. That is my illustration—drawn from Isaiah's imagery. It is a picture of what the saints of God are going to do on the resurrection morning.

Rise and sing, you who dwell in the dust!

I bow my head and continue to pray with the humble writer of the Revelation: "Amen! Come, Lord Jesus!"

# 3.

# The Appeal in Revelation: "Repent, and Be Faithful"

John to the seven churches which are in Asia: Grace be unto you, and peace, from him which is, and which was, and which is to come; and from the seven Spirits which are before his throne;

And from Jesus Christ, who is the faithful witness, and the first begotten of the dead, and the prince of the kings of the earth. Unto him that loved us, and washed us from our sins in his own blood,

And hath made us kings and priests unto God and his Father; to him be glory and dominion for ever and ever. Amen.

I was in the Spirit on the Lord's day, and heard behind me a great voice, as of a trumpet,

Saying, I am Alpha and Omega, the first and the last: and, What thou seest, write in a book, and send it unto the seven churches which are in Asia; unto Ephesus, and unto Smyrna, and unto Pergamos, and unto Thyatira, and unto Sardis, and unto Philadelphia, and unto Laodicea.

Revelation 1:4-6, 10, 11

The glorified Christ instructed John: "Write on a scroll what you see and send it to the . . . churches." The risen, eternal Christ of God uses the vision He gave to His servant John to transmit a message of warning and concern to every Christian congregation everywhere.

This call of Jesus to the Christian churches to prepare themselves for His return finds its basis in the total integrity of His promise. The Son of man is a person of His word. He said He would return, and He will. He will return to earth and every eye will see Him. Further, all the peoples of the earth will "mourn" because of Him. It will be a day of mourning, indeed, for those who did not prepare—for those who refused to believe that He meant what He said.

The more I study the Revelation, the more assured I am that Christ's love for His church is unchanging and eternal. We are barely into this Christ-centered prophecy before Jesus signifies how important the church is to Him.

Plainly, the living and eternal Head of the Christian church was not asking for some outward show of human perfection in His people. He was not appealing for a merely formal and classic kind of churchmanship— colorful pageantry, familiar ritual. Rather, His message was an appeal for brotherly love, for spiritual warmth, for genuine compassion. It was an expressed hope for sincere repentance, for renewal, for faithfulness among His forgiven, believing people, the children of God.

In the light of Christ's great love for His church, I have tried to review my own concerns for the churches of my pastoral ministry. I am aware that my critics say I have spoken too freely and openly about apathy, shallowness and worldliness in our Christian circles. I have asked myself—and I again ask the critics: "Are words of warning, correction and reproof something new in the Christian family?"

The question is rhetorical, of course. We already know the answer. It is an answer inherent in this divine message in the Revelation, addressed some 1,900 years ago to the Christian churches. The congregations named then have often been described as spiritually representative of all churches throughout the centuries of Christian history.

## Enough rope for Satan

Before I pursue that theme, however, let me speak of Satan's big mistake. We have a familiar saying, "Give a person enough rope and he will hang himself." Satan must have congratulated himself when he succeeded in having John shut away in the lonely isolation of exile. But the plot boomeranged. Instead of getting an obituary notice announcing John's death, the churches received messages of great encouragement and the outline of Christ's future victory. Satan should never have stirred up the Roman authorities to arrest and banish the saintly John. God allowed His faithful disciple to see farther from his island prison than any king has been able to see from his palace!

John wrote what he saw and what he heard concerning the heavenly scene. He detailed the judgments of God that would ultimately take place on earth. The messages he conveyed to the churches were brief but significant. Many eminent Bible scholars through the years have expressed their belief that the spiritual mountains and valleys of Christian church history are portrayed in the divine descriptions of both spiritual life and spiritual drought at Ephesus, Smyrna, Pergamum, Thyatira, Sardis, Philadelphia and Laodicea.

This raises a question often asked: Why were these messages directed to these seven churches? Why were not some of the older churches—those in Jerusalem, Antioch, Rome and Corinth, for instance—included?

We are finite, and we do not know the reasons. But we do accept the fact that the Spirit of God was dictating a special message that would ultimately convey God's burden to the entire Christian community throughout the world. And we know from its use elsewhere in the Bible that the number seven suggests wholeness and completeness. The fact that seven churches were selected speaks of the possibility that the seven so named were indeed representative examples of the entire believing body of Christ on the earth.

## They were familiar to John

These Asia Minor churches were especially dear to John. No doubt he had assisted in their founding and for years had lovingly nurtured their spiritual growth. There is indication in extra-biblical sources that John had made Ephesus his adopted city and in his home there had cared for Mary, Jesus' mother, until her death.

What of the messages to these seven churches? Let us consider their highlights.

To the church at Ephesus Jesus gave this word: "Thou hast left thy first love. Remember therefore from whence thou art fallen" (2:4-5). To Smyrna, Jesus had this instruction: "Be faithful, even to the point of death, and I will give you the crown of life" (2:10).

Jesus had a rebuke for the church at Pergamum: "But I have a few things against thee . . . Repent . . .!" (2:14, 16). At Thyatira, wrong teaching and evil conduct were to be repudiated. The Savior said, "All the churches shall know that I am he which searcheth the reins and hearts: and I will give unto every one of you according to your works" (2:23).

Jesus commanded the church at Sardis to rouse itself. "I know thy works, that thou hast a name that thou livest, and art dead. Be watchful!" (3:1-2). The One "who is holy and true" had encouragement for the church in Philadelphia: "Because thou hast kept the word of my patience, I also will keep thee from the hour of temptation, which shall come upon all the world, to try them that dwell upon the earth" (3:10). His final message was to the church at Laodicea: "I know thy works, that thou art neither cold nor hot: I would thou wert cold or hot. So then because thou art lukewarm, and neither cold nor hot, I will spue thee out of my mouth" (3:15-16).

From these brief summaries, it is apparent that even in that early period of church history, congregations were in need of reproof—and encouragement. Thankfully, a God of love and provision knows how to give both. In these messages we see the wise authority and loving direction of the Head of the church. In no better way could we be given a sweeping view of what Christianity is—and what the churches are all about.

## Understanding Christianity

There are many definitions of Christianity in our day. Most of them are woefully weak because they lack the authority of God's revelation in His Word. Christianity is not just another religious persuasion as defined by groups of religious leaders in Rome or Geneva, in New York City or Toronto. Christianity is actually what the Holy Spirit claimed it to be in the Scriptures. It is what the prophets of God, the seers and sages and apostles said it was as they were moved by the Holy Spirit to speak and to write.

This is the Christian life and Christian witness we accepted when we became Christians by sincere faith in God's Word. Here is the beating heart of the holy faith that will take us home to heaven and to God. Here is our heart interest and here is our hope for the eternal future.

As John portrays the true meaning of the Christian faith in the churches, he relates everything to God, the Father, who was and who is and who is to come; to the sevenfold Spirit of God who proceeds from the Father; and to Jesus Christ, the eternal Son, our Savior and Lord. The entire declaration to the churches rings with the certainty of the ultimate triumph to come.

Although there is enough spiritual and doctrinal teaching in these first three chapters of the Revelation for a dozen books, I want at this time to emphasize just two things: (1) the divine authority given to our Lord Jesus Christ and (2) the power and the illumination the church needs to receive from the Holy Spirit. I will also briefly mention a doctrine that is not always recognized: the dominion of the saints—really, the authority given to the believing children of God.

First, John mentions the two treasures, grace and peace, that God has willed to those who believe and obey (1:4). He designates grace and peace as coming to us, men and women in fellowship with God. John makes a benediction of these two spiritual treasures. Then he fashions a wonderful doxology: to Jesus Christ belongs "glory and dominion for ever and ever" (1:6).

Benediction literally means "the good word." Doxology means "the word of praise." Taken together, the two put things in their right places: grace and peace for us believing men and women; glory and power for the God who has loved us to the point of death. What a frightful, grotesque situation it would be both in heaven and on earth if those roles were reversed! We cannot imagine a time and situation in which our God would need grace and peace—or in which we humans should be accorded glory and power for ever and ever.

No, the roles and the positions are correctly stated. Why would we ever need more for our wretched sinfulness than the grace of God? What more do we need for our poor, uprooted, alienated, distraught souls than peace?

## Beyond grace and peace: love

The Holy Spirit then helps us recognize the kind of love we received from Jesus Christ, who has freed us from our sins by His blood. Have you yet learned that love is not a thing of reason? Love tries to be reasonable, but it seldom succeeds. There is a sweet wisdom in love that is above reason—it rises above it and goes far beyond it. Who could ever imagine the God of all the universe condensing Himself into human form and, out of His love, dying for His alienated people? It seems an unreasonable thing to do, but it was reasonable in that it was the supreme wisdom of the mighty God!

The saintly Lady Julian, centuries ago, cherished this love that is ours in Christ. She wrote: "Out of His goodness, God made us. Out of His goodness, He keeps us. When man had sinned, He redeemed us again out of His goodness. Then do you not suppose that God will give His children the best of everything out of His goodness?"

But on to the divine authority ascribed to Jesus Christ, the eternal Son. Three things are said of Him here. He is the faithful witness, which means He is God's prophet. He is the firstborn from the dead, which speaks of His priesthood. And He is the ruler of the kings of the earth, which implies His kingship. This is the ageless revelation from God concerning His Christ. Jesus our Lord is Prophet, Priest and King. The concept is not new, yet many preachers never preach it and many congregations never hear it.

Jesus was God's faithful witness. In effect He said: "I am a reporter. I have come down from heaven, and the things that I saw there I speak to you. I tell you the truth, but you will not receive it." He was the Prophet of all prophets, the summation of all of God's prophets.

But He was more. His ministry was that of the priest of God. He offered Himself. He was the only priest in all of history who could offer Himself as an offering and a sacrifice to God. The writer to the Hebrews says clearly that "Christ . . . through the eternal Spirit offered himself without spot to God" (9:14). Then God raised Him from the dead, and He is now our great High Priest at the right hand of God.

> Where high the heavenly temple stands,
> The house of God not made with hands,
> The great High Priest our nature wears,
> The Guardian of mankind appears.

## Jesus is a glorified Man

Let this truth penetrate. There is a glorified Human Being at the right hand of God—not a spirit but a Man glorified. He is there interceding for us, representing us. This is why I believe in the security of the saints. How can I help but believe that? If Jesus Christ is at the right hand of God, then He has invested Himself—charged Himself—with full authority, authority given Him by God the Father. My name is on His multistone breast-piece (see Exodus 39:8-14), and I am safe!

Someone once asked Dr. Graham Scroggie, "Are you a Calvinist?" I feel Dr. Scroggie was speaking for me when he replied, "When I am on my knees praying, I am a Calvinist. But when I get into the pulpit to preach, I am an Arminian!" That my great High Priest will keep me, I have no doubt. Will He do so because of my goodness? No! Will He keep you because of your goodness? Again, no! We are kept because He is at the throne of God interceding for us.

Jesus Christ is also Ruler over all the kings of the earth, and we await His day of consummation and triumph when every knee shall bow before Him "of things in heaven, and things in earth, and things under the earth; and that every tongue should confess that Jesus Christ is Lord, to the glory of God the Father" (Philippians 2:10-11).

## A question for the church

There is a question that should be answered in every Christian church: Are we honoring the Holy Spirit of God? That is, are we allowing Him to do what He wants to do in our midst today?

More than once in the Revelation John mentions the seven-fold Spirit of God and His presence before the heavenly throne. In the Old Testament, the prophet Isaiah describes his stirring vision of this same Spirit, who was to be God's presence, wisdom, understanding, counsel, might, knowledge and reverence in the life of the expected Messiah (Isaiah 11:1-3). Jesus did not begin His earthly ministry until at His water baptism the living Spirit of God had become all of those things to Him.

I have reason to suspect that many people are trying to give leadership in Christian churches today without ever having yielded to the wise and effective leading of the Holy Spirit. He truly is the Spirit of wisdom, understanding and counsel. He alone can bring the gracious presence of the living God into our lives and ministries.

You may think it out of place for me to say so, but in our churches today we are leaning too heavily upon human talents and educated abilities. We forget that the illumination of the Holy Spirit of God is a necessity, not only in our ministerial preparation, but in the administrative and leadership functions of our churches.

We need an enduement of the Spirit of God! We sorely need more of His wisdom, His counsel, His power, His knowledge. We need to reverence and fear the Almighty God. If we knew the full provision and the spiritual anointing that Jesus promised through the Holy Spirit, we would be far less dependent on so many other things.

Psychiatrists, psychologists, anthropologists, sociologists—and most of the other "ologists"—have their place in our society. I do not doubt that. But many of these professionals now have credentials in the church, and I fear that their counsel is put above the ministry of the Holy Spirit. I have said it before, and I say it now: We need the Holy Spirit more and more, and we need human helps less and less!

## We shall have dominion

There is a further beautiful emphasis within John's opening benediction and ascription of praise to God. We identify it as the doctrine of the dominion of the saints. John says this eternal Prophet, Priest and King not only "has freed us from our sins by his blood," but in addition He "hath made us kings and priests unto God and his Father" (Revelation 1:5-6). We have greater authority than we know—and greater authority than we ever exercise!

There is an amazing provision for Christian believers in our daily encounters and conflicts with Satan, the enemy of our souls. I cannot agree with those optimistic people who try to dismiss Satan as a figment of the imagination. They are wrong. There is a real devil. But we do not have to be afraid of him if we know and exercise the dominion and authority of the saints of God.

The Bible tells us that Satan is a real personality. He has a distinct history behind him. We dare to face and resist him in the authority that comes to us from heaven. John tells us that our authority comes from Jesus Christ, who has made His believing saints to be a kingdom and priests in His service.

God holds no mental reservations about any of us when we become His children by faith. When He forgives us, He trusts us as though we had never sinned. When Satan comes around to taunt me about my past sins, I remind him that everything that had been charged against me came from him, and now everything I have—forgiveness and peace and freedom—I have freely received from my Lord Jesus Christ!

As long as you remain on this earth, God has not completed His work in you. The Spirit of God will help you discern when the chastening hand of God is upon you. But if it is the devil trying to tamper with your Christian life and testimony, dare to resist him in the victorious power of the living Christ.

This great truth is related to the fact that Jesus is our eternal High Priest, now exalted at the throne of God. He has said to us, "Whatever your need, just come to the throne of grace. Anything you need, you may have!" Why not believe Him and exercise the dominion He has given you?

There is no reason for any of us to hide or to slink about as if we must get permission to exist. As children of God, we need not apologize for walking around in God's earth. Christ has made us a kingdom of believer-priests. This is a fact, a Bible doctrine. We are priests. We have the right as believer-priests to go direct to our great High Priest in the heavens, making our legitimate wants and wishes known to Him. He has promised to intercede for us at the heavenly throne.

## Why do so few respond?

The dominion of the saints is an encouraging, uplifting truth. Why, then, does not everyone know about it and respond? Indeed, why do millions of men and women not respond to the grace and love of God? Has "the god of this world . . . blinded the minds of them which believe not, lest the light of the glorious gospel of Christ, who is the image of God, should shine unto them" (2 Corinthians 4:4)?

The proponents of universalism twist certain Bible verses to make them the saving umbrella for the whole human race. But Scripture forbids such a conclusion, and reason forbids it. The promises are for the Lord's people—for those who are His by faith, those who love and serve Him.

There is no other way than the faith way. Everyone—every man and every woman—must decide whether he or she will be included under this gracious benediction from God the Father or excluded from claiming it!

# 4.

# The Portrait in Revelation: "The Eternal Christ!"

"I John, who also am your brother, and companion in tribulation, and in the kingdom and patience of Jesus Christ, was in the isle that is called Patmos, for the word of God, and for the testimony of Jesus Christ . . ."

"And I turned to see the voice that spake with me. And being turned, I saw seven golden candlesticks; and in the midst of the seven candlesticks one like unto the Son of man, clothed with a garment down to the foot, and girt about the paps with a golden girdle. His head and his hairs were white like wool, as white as snow; and his eyes were as a flame of fire; And his feet like unto fine brass, as if they burned in a furnace; and his voice as the sound of many waters. And he had in his right hand seven stars: and out of his mouth went a sharp twoedged sword: and his countenance was as the sun shineth in his strength . . ."

"The mystery of the seven stars which thou sawest in my right hand, and the seven golden candlesticks. The seven stars are the angels of the seven churches: and the

> seven candlesticks which thou sawest are the seven
> churches."
>
> Revelation 1:9, 12-16, 20

All of the great artists of the past, all of them combining their talents on a gigantic canvas, could never have given us a true portrait of our Lord Jesus Christ or of His universal power. Instead, we look into the Scriptures, and particularly into the Revelation, to find a satisfying description of the eternal Son of God with whom we will be associated throughout the ages to come.

William T. MacArthur, an early leader in The Christian and Missionary Alliance and one of its outstanding preachers, termed the description of Jesus Christ in Revelation 1:13-16 "the only authentic portrait of our Savior and Lord."

Those celebrated European painters, whose works adorn the world's great art galleries, undoubtedly did their best to depict our Lord. They were limited, however, by their finite concepts of the Subject. To be frank, I do not want to hold in my mind an unworthy concept of my divine Savior. We Christians should earnestly desire the Holy Spirit to sketch a true and transforming portrait of Jesus Christ across our innermost beings! Our delight should be in the assurance that Christ lives within us, moment by moment. And that assurance must come from God's holy Word.

Do you personally desire with me that the Holy Spirit will dip His brush and begin to paint across the canvas of our souls a living portrayal of Jesus Christ, complete with blood and fire?

It is a sad thought, but I suppose some Christians are going to be disappointed when they actually see Jesus. Their concept of Him has been shaped by the paintings and images they have seen of the human Jesus. The

radiant, awesome Jesus of the Revelation is totally out-
side their perspective.

Those who are critical of the Scriptures would have us
believe that the symbols in the Revelation are meaning-
less and a study in futility. I take strong exception to
such conclusions! John saw much, he learned much, and
he shares his understanding. For example, Jesus
explained to John that the seven stars in His right hand
are the angels of the seven churches, and the seven
lampstands are the seven churches. John passes on that
information to us.


## Valuable insights

In detailing his vision of the risen, glorified Christ, John
conveys valuable insights to us. Jesus' vesture is the
priestly robe. His golden sash is designed for royalty.
His snow-white head and hair speak of God's utter holiness. His eyes, "as a flame of fire," and his feet, "like
unto fine brass, as if they burned in a furnace," depict
God's wrath and judgment. John saw the face of Jesus as
the sun shining in its full strength. How can anyone add
to that? If you want to know how strong the sun is, try
looking into the sky at midday. You never, never can
gaze directly into that full glow.

But we are Jesus' disciples, and we think of another
time and another scene when Jesus' "visage was so
marred more than any man, and his form more than the
sons of men" (Isaiah 52:14). It was a time when "he hath
no form nor comeliness; and when we shall see him,
there is no beauty that we should desire him" (Isaiah
53:2-3).

Yes, this Jesus Christ had come to live among us and
to give His life a ransom for the sins of a lost world. Evil

men took Him and said, "We know how to deal with Him." They beat Him with their whips and bruised Him with their fists. They tore at His beard, leaving His countenance marred and bleeding. In final insult, they spit in His holy face. Yet, as He bled and died on a Roman cross, He cried out in prayer, "Father, forgive them; for they know not what they do" (Luke 23:34).

As one of the redeemed and forgiven, I can better understand Isaiah's portrait of the suffering Savior, the Servant of Jehovah. I know He was willing to die in my place. But in John's vision, Jesus is the Overcomer, the One who was dead but now is alive for ever and ever. I cannot fully comprehend the power and the glory belonging to this One whose face will shine eternally with the brilliance of the sun! I do not have the words to explain that kind of brightness and light.

## Jesus created everything

Our scientists explain to us how the sun daily gives us light, heat and health, all the while providing energy and a variety of necessary elements that are absorbed into the earth. Then we dig and probe to release the oil, gas and coal that the sun has helped to make. We put them in our combustion chambers so that our cars and trains and ships and planes can traverse the world.

John portrays the Man who made it all, the One whose face shines with the brilliance and energy of the sun. "The Man who made it all?" you ask, puzzled. Yes! Hear what the apostle Paul says of Jesus Christ: "He is the image of the invisible God, the firstborn of every creature: for by him were all things created, that are in heaven, and that are in earth, visible and invisible, whether they be thrones, or dominions, or principalities, or powers: all things were created by him, and for him" (Colossians 1:15-16).

Some may doubt this fact, but for the gospel's sake— and because Scripture clearly states it—we must assert that they are wrong. We must stand up to those who would belittle Jesus Christ. We must take issue with those who question that John saw and tried to describe the eternity, the majesty, the glory, the power and the final authority of Jesus Christ, our Lord. As for me, I am positive about this Revelation God has given to His believing children!

## No stranger to suffering

John was well aware of Satan's attack against God and the church in that first century of Christian history. He humbly affirmed that he was a "companion in tribulation, and in the kingdom and patience of Jesus Christ" (Revelation 1:9). And what had John's faithful Christian testimony earned for him? Exile!

Had it happened in North American in our era, some publisher would have flown in to offer John a five- or six-figure check for book rights to his story. But I do not think John would have been concerned about turning a personal financial profit from his experience. The present-day financial value of a "born again testimony" was mercifully unknown in A.D. 95.

"Give your heart to the Lord, get born again, and your business will grow and grow and grow!" "If you want to become a top athlete and well known, just accept the Lord and be born again!" "If you want your cows to give more milk . . ." "If you want to be sure of getting better grades in college . . ."

Possibly no one ever had a clearer, sweeter, stronger testimony of the grace and salvation that is in Jesus Christ than John. Humbly he relates it: "I . . . [am] your brother and companion in . . . tribulation . . . [I] was in the isle that is called Patmos, for the word of God and for the testimony of Jesus Christ."

In our day, the media would be asking, "What are you doing there on Patmos, John? You were the bishop at Ephesus. You should be at home among your people, presiding over your congregation. You were born again, were you not, John?"

"Yes," John would have replied meekly, "I was the Lord's disciple and companion, and I have been ministering and witnessing as He said. I am now His servant in exile."

Allow me to be frank about this insidious issue in our Christian circles. If the modern doctrine of "accepting Jesus" is all its current advocates claim it to be, John would not have been suffering in a one-man slave camp on Patmos. He would be at home with his congregation. He would have financial prosperity. He would know what strings to pull and how to be friendly with the right people in high places.

## But no Revelation

Remember this, however: If John had been a product of our present-day "accept Jesus and prosper" gospel, he would have seen no divine vision of Christ's glory and coming triumph; he would have written no Revelation. John could have chosen to compromise his faith. Had he done so, he would have remained at home—balancing his praise between God and Caesar. But then he never would have glimpsed that open door in heaven or the throne with the heavenly rainbow encircling it.

Yes, John could have taken the easier way. Just a little compromise and the important people would begin to say, "This man is really doing good things for the community." But John was a man of faith. He knew what he believed; he knew in whom he believed. He was willing to take the heat from those who hated the living God and His Christ.

If you are willing to lower the temperature of your testimony, the world will turn off the heat it has been applying. But if you are faithful to God and His Word, consistent and sincere in your testimony to what Christ means to you, you can expect both heat and pressure. John had a strong, uncompromising testimony. It evoked the opposition of the powers, who decided to silence his witness in Patmos's rocky isolation.

There is a spiritual lesson for us in John's response to the voice of the living Christ. He says, "And I turned to see the voice that spake with me" (1:12). John was not the first person to hear the Lord's voice behind him. Does this say to us that we are usually facing the wrong way?

The prophet Isaiah knew full well that Israel had turned her back on God, departing from His way. He counseled, "And thine ears shall hear a word behind thee, saying, This is the way, walk ye in it, when ye turn to the right hand, and when ye turn to the left" (Isaiah 30:21). Let us be thankful for God's mercy and patience. He is the only One who is always faithful, always loyal, always compassionate. His voice continues to call, "Come! Turn back! Walk in My way!"

John says he turned and saw someone "like unto the Son of man." His vision was that of our Lord and His presence in the midst of the churches. In our time we have all kinds of status symbols in the Christian church —membership, attendance, pastoral staff, missionary offerings. But there is only one status symbol that should make a Christian congregation genuinely glad. That is to know that our Lord is present, walking in our midst!

## Our real need

Some Christians say they need a great cathedral if they are to properly worship—or a mighty organ or artistic, stained-glass windows. Do not be concerned about those outward symbols. Just be sure you have gladly welcomed into your midst the One whose eyes are like a flame of fire, the One from whose mouth proceeds a double-edged sword—the Word of God.

Some time ago I was invited to visit and preach in a smaller church in Toronto. I found a group of dear people—a humble, ethnic assembly. Many of them could not speak good, standard English. But their faith and joy in knowing Christ warmed my heart. After the service, they called for a prayer meeting, and I want to tell you that it was an experience I will never forget!

No matter the size of the assembly or its other attributes, our Lord wants it to be known by His presence in the midst. I would rather have His presence in the church than anything else in all the wide world.

Hearing the proud manner in which some speak of the high dollar cost of their sanctuaries, must lead people to suppose that spirituality can be purchased. But the secret of true spiritual worship is to discern and know the presence of the living Christ in our midst.

One further thought: John turned and saw someone "like unto the Son of man' "in the midst of the churches. John did not see a spirit. He saw a Man—a glorified Man, the Son of man, our Lord Jesus Christ, clad in a priestly garment and wearing the golden sash of royalty. He was not a spirit, not an angel, not a cherubim. He was a real Man—a priest with royal insignia, bringing to mind again the designation of the eternal Son as Prophet, Priest and King. He stands in the midst of the churches.

Does that not explain much about the life and faithfulness of Christian churches? Many have their difficulties. Many have known the path of backsliding. Satan brings his pressures to bear on weaknesses in the church. If it were not for the presence of our Lord and Savior in the midst, there would be no church! God's presence is the only reason for its existence.

In John's portrayal, the Son of man had feet like bronze, glowing as if in a fire. This is the language and symbolism of judgment, and our Lord is to be Judge. The church that accepts no judgment is not the church of our Lord Jesus Christ. It cannot be Christ's church if our risen and glorified Lord is not the center of all its interests.

## The church must be holy

The true church understands that it must live a disciplined life. Although our High Priest loves us in spite of our weaknesses and failures, He encourages us to be a holy people because He is a holy God. Holiness may be an unpopular subject in some churches, but holiness in the Christian life is a precious treasure in God's sight.

What I say here may hurt, but I say it anyhow. We have lived with unholiness so long that we are almost incapable of recognizing true holiness. The people of God in the churches of Jesus Christ ought to be a holy people. But ministers have largely given up preaching Bible-centered sermons on holiness. Maybe they would not know what to do with hearers who fell under the convicting power of God's Word. Preachers today would rather give their congregations tranquilizers.

I preach to my congregation week after week. And I pray that I may be able to preach with such convicting power that my people will sweat! I do not want them to leave my services feeling good. The last thing I want to do is to give them some kind of religious tranquilizer— and let them go to hell in their relaxation.

The Christian church was designed to make sinners sweat. I have always believed that, and I still believe it. The messages preached in our churches should make backslidden Christians sweat. And if I achieve that objective when I preach, I thank God with all of my heart, no matter what people think of me.

Our Lord is a holy Lord, and His eyes are as a flame of fire. His X-ray eyes can see right through everything! We can hide nothing from God. He sees all and knows all. But apparently we have a hard time with that fact—preachers and lay people alike. We seem to think our respectability should be accepted by our Lord as spirituality. That is the same tragic mistake the self-righteous Pharisees made in Jesus' day. We like to imagine we are important, and we like to hear people talking about our importance. But every one of us is going to die one of these days. There will be a funeral service and then we will be buried, just like everybody else.

## God already knows all about us

God knows everything about me better than I know it myself. He knows that my humility is only another form of pride. He knows that! And I am glad He does. Some people have an idea the devil may tattle some scandal about them to God. They forget that God already knows all there is to know about them.

I am glad God knows all He knows. No one is going to seek out our Lord and whisper behind his or her hand, "Have you heard the latest about Tozer?" Jesus already knows everything there is to know about me. He knows my strengths and He knows my weaknesses. And He has already told us that the only thing capable of harming us is to believe we can do all things in our own strength.

We can never get too weak for the Lord to use us—but we can get too strong, if it is our own strength. We can never be too ignorant for the Lord to use us—but we can be too wise in our own conceit. We can never get too small for the Lord to use us, but we can surely get too big and get in His way.

The Christian church dares not settle for anything less than the illumination of the Holy Spirit and the presence of our divine Prophet, Priest and King in our midst. Let us never be led into the mistake that so many are making—sighing and saying, "Oh, if we only had bigger, wiser men in our pulpits! Oh, if we only had more important men in places of Christian leadership!"

In John's vision, the sharp, double-edged sword proceeded out of the mouth of the Son of man. All other swords will fail and vanish, but the sharp sword, the Word of the Lord, will prevail. By all means, we had better stay with the sharp sword of His Word.

How terrible it is to simply go on playing in God's presence. How human it is to sleep and dream in God's presence. What a tragedy when we sin in His presence. Jesus our Lord is in our midst. He is here. Now. And we are a people getting ready to see Him face to face.

Are we ready for that face-to-face encounter?

# 5.

# The Call To Worship in Revelation: "Holy, Holy, Holy!"

After this I looked, and, behold, a door was opened in heaven: and the first voice which I heard was as it were of a trumpet talking with me; which said, Come up hither, and I will shew thee things which must be hereafter. And immediately I was in the spirit: and, behold, a throne was set in heaven, and one sat on the throne . . . Also before the throne there was what looked like a sea of glass, clear as crystal.

And before the throne there was a sea of glass like unto crystal: and in the midst of the throne, and round about the throne, were four beasts full of eyes before and behind. And the first beast was like a lion, and the second beast like a calf, and the third beast had a face as a man, and the fourth beast was like a flying eagle. And the four beasts had each of them six wings about him; and they were full of eyes within: and they rest not day and night, saying,

Holy, holy, holy, Lord God Almighty, which was, and is, and is to come.

And when those beasts give glory and honour and thanks to him that sat on the throne, who liveth for ever and ever, The four and twenty elders fall down before him that sat on the throne, and worship him that liveth for ever and ever, and cast their crowns before the throne, saying,

> Thou art worthy, O LORD, to receive glory and honour and power:
> for thou hast created all things, and for thy pleasure they are and were created.

Revelation 4:1-2, 6-11

What a moving thought it is to learn that in the heavenly realm God receives unceasing worship from the living creatures surrounding His throne! "They rest not day and night, saying:

> "Holy, holy, holy,
> LORD God Almighty,
> which was, and is, and is to come"

(Revelation 4:8).

As John glimpsed the majesty and holiness of God in this heavenly scene, he was overwhelmed by what he saw and heard. It must have been like trying to pour an ocean into a teacup—and John staggered under the revelation! He had to try to describe the indescribable, and he lacked both language and reference points to do so. But he recognized the unceasing worship ascribed to God the Father around His heavenly throne.

Looking at what John wrote, I wonder how so many present-day Christians can consider an hour of worship Sunday morning as adequate adoration of the holy God who created them and then redeemed them back to

Himself. I have been at funerals where the presiding minister preached the deceased right into heaven. Yet the earthly life of the departed plainly said that he or she would be bored to tears in a heavenly environment of continuous praise and adoration of God.

This is personal opinion, but I do not think death is going to transform our attitudes and disposition. If in this life we are not really comfortable talking or singing about heaven, I doubt that death will transform us into enthusiasts. If the worship and adoration of God are tedious now, they will be tedious after the hour of death. I do not know that God is going to force any of us into His heaven. I doubt that He will say to any of us, "You were never interested in worshiping Me while you were on earth, but in heaven I am going to make that your greatest interest and your ceaseless occupation!"

Controversial? Perhaps. But I am trying to stir you up, to encourage you to delight in a life of praise and spiritual victory! God is pleased with His people when His praise is continually and joyfully on their lips. The heavenly scene John describes is the unceasing cry of the adoring living creatures, "Holy, holy, holy!" They rest not, day or night. My fear is that too many of God's professing people down here are resting far too often between their efforts at praise.

## The elders and the "creatures"

Turning again to John's vision, we learn that surrounding the throne of God were 24 other thrones, and seated on them were 24 elders. They were dressed in white robes, and they had crowns of gold on their heads. Then John describes four "living creatures" covered with eyes, each having six wings. John says that when these four living creatures ascribe glory, honor and thanks to God, the 24 elders fall down before God and worship Him. The elders lay their crowns before the throne and say, "You created all things. You are worthy to receive glory and honor and power."

Do we know the symbolism of these 24 elders? No. The Scriptures do not make it clear. But I am going to tell you how I have come to view these worshipping elders. I think 12 of them probably represent the overcomers in Israel and 12 of them represent the overcomers in the church. To say it another way, 12 represent the 12 tribes of Israel; 12 represent the 12 apostles of Jesus Christ.

Do you recall Peter's remark during one of his conversations with Jesus? "Behold, we have forsaken all, and followed thee; what shall we have therefore?" (Matthew 19:27). Jesus responded with this statement: "Verily I say unto you, That ye which have followed me, in the regeneration when the Son of man shall sit in the throne of his glory, ye also shall sit upon twelve thrones, judging the twelve tribes of Israel." The thrones Jesus mentions may not be the ones John saw, but Jesus' words were certainly definite about the apostles sitting on 12 thrones in that coming day.

John also saw four "living creatures." You may recall that they were termed "beasts" in the King James Version. I think "living creatures" is a better translation because they were not "beastly" creatures. Again, we sympathize with John as he tries to describe heavenly creatures in human terms. It was impossible for God to fully reveal Himself and the heavenly glories to John. How can the Infinite be fully perceived by finite, mortal man?

God had to impose some sort of a veil. If God had suddenly revealed Himself fully to John, the apostle would have perished as an autumn leaf disappears in a blazing fire. No mortal can look into the blaze of God's full glory and live! So John is attempting to tell us what he discerns in the vision of the four heavenly beings at the throne of God.

## The four living creatures

The first living creature was like a lion. The second was like an ox. The third had the face of a man. The fourth was like a soaring eagle. Lion—king of beasts. Ox—beast of burden. Man—what we are. Flying eagle—at home in the heavens. Do you perceive a larger picture developing? Did you know that for centuries Christians have seen these same "faces" in the four Gospels of the New Testament? Matthew's is the gospel of the King. Mark's, the gospel of the suffering Servant. Luke's, the gospel of the Son of man. John's, the gospel of the Son of God.

God has put Jesus Christ's picture everywhere! Four living, immortal creatures before the throne. Four loving, adoring, worshipping beings, faithfully and forever devoted to the purpose of praising God and the eternal Son, the Lamb of God who takes away the sin of the world!

Make no mistake about it. The imagery is plainly the gospel of Christ. He is what Christianity is all about.

The characteristics of the lion are power and dominion. The lion is king. The glory of a king does not lie in his own person but rather in the character of his people. The glory of this noble and kingly Person, Christ Jesus, pictured as the lion, lies in the fact that He rules a people who are supremely and perfectly happy.

The ox is the willing burden-bearer, obedient even to sacrifice. In the Old Testament system, there was little for the ox to look forward to except sacrifice, blood and death. The ox is a symbol of God's great plan of atonement and redemption through Jesus Christ.

The third being, John testified, had a face like a man. The symbolism of the Son continues, for Jesus became Man and lived among us that He might die for us: "For even the Son of man came not to be ministered unto, but to minister, and to give his life a ransom for many" (Mark 10:45).

Finally, the eagle like fourth living creature was a flying, soaring being. Earth may be the eagle's resting place, but the heavens are its habitat. Jesus was the Son of man, partaking of our humanity, but He was also the Son of God—"very God of very God," as the fathers phrased it in the Nicene creed.

## Are we walking in the light?

What have we been doing with all the light and guidance God has given us in His Word and through His Spirit? I am concerned that some Christian leaders are deriding the "mysticism" of spiritually minded Christian believers—men and women who are so devoted to Jesus Christ that nothing else in this life and in this world much matters.

A couple of generations ago, all Christendom was in one of two camps: People were either "liberals" (also called "modernists" and "rationalists"), who questioned the inspired authority of the Scriptures and who denied that Jesus was more than a master teacher and a splendid human example. Or people were "evangelicals"— accepting without question the fundamental and total authority of the Scriptures as God's Spirit-inspired Word and recognizing Jesus Christ as God enfleshed. Now, suddenly, we find the lines are no longer so simply drawn. Now an increasing number of scholars and authors claim to be both evangelicals and rationalists.

Church history is clear. Jesus Christ has always had devoted, adoring followers who found it possible to love their Savior and Lord with all their hearts and minds and souls. If so-called evangelicals can now speak lightly about these "evangelical mystics," we must conclude that truth in our day has taken a cruelly cynical twist.

Those evangelical mystics have been a potent force for God and for the Word of God. You will have to count Moses, David, Isaiah, John and Paul among them. You will have to count Augustine, Luther and the Wesleys. You will have to add Lady Julian, Fanny Crosby, Francis Faber, Brother Lawrence, A.B. Simpson and a mighty host of other men and women whose greatest delight in life was the rapturous love of God in their souls!

Could it be that in our advanced generation we are forgetting that all people will have to answer to God for the decisions they made in life either accepting or rejecting the spiritual light God has given them? Are we forgetting that the moral judgments of God will fall upon individuals and nations according to the light they have received?

## Degrees of punishment

The Bible is plain: "And that servant, which knew his lord's will, and prepared not himself, neither did according to his will, shall be beaten with many stripes. But he that knew not, and did commit things worthy of stripes, shall be beaten with few stripes" (Luke 12:47-48). God is a merciful God, but He is also holy and just. I do not believe, as some do, that God will find a way to bring everyone to heaven in the last day. But in His justice and fairness He has provided many warnings and cautions in the Scriptures about the spiritual light and spiritual responsibilities He has given us. They are directed to us all.

John saw the flashes of lightning. He felt the peals of rumbling thunder. He heard the mighty voices and the trumpet blasts as the angels of God held back the soon-to-be-released judgments coming upon the earth and the seas. We look around us, and we see this world's cup of iniquity brim full. One day, when it reaches the point of overflow, God will say, "Enough! Open the seals! Sound the trumpets of judgment!"

The justice of God and the wrath of God have been ignored and violated so long and so arrogantly that the day of reckoning must come. The divine lightning, the peals of thunder and the rumbling of judgment will go out from the throne.

Some who have misconstrued the meaning of God's grace will make light of such predictions. But the Bible is unequivocal: God's throne of grace will become a throne of judgment.

I confess that I am stirred within my being as I study these portions of the Revelation. If I were not a Christian, saved and forgiven, I would not wait. I would get down on my knees and plead for God's grace and mercy while there is time. I would not deceive my own soul with the excuse that "I do not have enough light" or "I do not understand all that Christ did" or "Why am I any worse in God's sight than my neighbor?"

## They are only excuses

It is sad but true that many people are going to hell while they try to hide behind a variety of excuses. As a minister, I have never found men and women rejecting the gospel of Christ on the basis of misunderstanding or confusion. Rather, the problem is some dark place in the soul, some secret sin. The rejection of Christ is the refusal to give these things up and come to the light of Christ and follow Him.

I for one never want to be in the tragic condition of living where the light of God cannot reach me. The world of nature has its flatworms and silverfish and other slimy creepers and crawlers. All of these try desperately to stay out of the light. They can only exist by avoiding the light of the sun. They live under the rocks and in the dark caves and the damp crevices. The last thing they desire is the glorious radiance of the sun. For us, the rays of the sun are part of God's bountiful provision for life and health, but the sun's rays cannot penetrate the hiding places of those creeping, crawling creatures.

I do not want to be like a hidden-away flatworm. I want to live in the light of God's grace and Spirit. Only in that way can I learn more of His love and of His person and character. Though I sense that God has already taught me much, I know there is still much more to be learned. God wants to give me more light, more understanding of His will and His ways. This is a great and far-reaching truth. John expressed it better than I can when he said:

> God is light, and in him is no darkness at all. If we say that we have fellowship with him, and walk in darkness, we lie, and do not the truth: But if we walk in the light, as he is in the light, we have fellowship one with another, and the blood of Jesus Christ his Son cleanseth us from all sin (1 John 1:5-7).

A serious-minded young man once talked with me. "Dr. Tozer," he said, "I know that every one of us was brought into this world with a design for life and for existence. Why are there so many among us who seem to be drifting, so many with no purpose in life and with no thought of eternity?"

No person can answer such a searching question for someone else! But I have analyzed it for myself and for my own life. If I should have missed—rejected—God's plan of salvation, it would have been far better for me to have been carried from my mother's arms to the grave while I was yet an unnamed infant. If I miss this gracious salvation, I miss the privilege of one day standing around the throne of God with the redeemed of all ages.

## Who is to be blamed?

And if I miss the love and the mercy and the grace of God in this life, who is to be blamed? Certainly not the God who sits on the throne. He made full provision for my salvation. Certainly not the Lamb who stands before the throne. He died for my sins and rose again for my justification. Certainly not the radiant, flaming Holy Spirit who has accosted men and women all over the world, mediating to them the saving gospel of Christ.

Hear the words John heard on rocky Patmos as the Revelation of Jesus Christ concluded:

> "And, behold, I come quickly; and my reward is with me, to give every man according as his work shall be . . .

> "Blessed are they that do his commandments, that they may have right to the tree of life, and may enter in through the gates into the city . . ."

"And the Spirit and the bride say, Come. And let him that heareth say, Come. And let him that is athirst come. And whosoever will, let him take the water of life freely." (22:12, 14, 17)

If I miss God's great salvation, has this life been worth the struggle? Personally, I think not!

# 6.

# The Title Deed in Revelation: "Worthy Is the Lamb!"

And I saw in the right hand of him that sat on the throne a book written within and on the backside, sealed with seven seals. And I saw a strong angel proclaiming with a loud voice, Who is worthy to open the book, and to loose the seals thereof? And no man in heaven, nor in earth, neither under the earth, was able to open the book, neither to look thereon. And I wept much, because no man was found worthy to open and to read the book, neither to look thereon. And one of the elders saith unto me, Weep not: behold, the Lion of the tribe of Judah, the Root of David, hath prevailed to open the book, and to loose the seven seals thereof. And I beheld, and, lo, in the midst of the throne and of the four beasts, and in the midst of the elders, stood a Lamb as it had been slain, having seven horns and seven eyes, which are the seven Spirits of God sent forth into all the earth. And he came and took the book out of the right hand of him that sat upon the throne. And when he had taken the book, the four beasts and four and twenty elders fell down before the Lamb, having every one of them harps, and golden vials full of odours, which are the prayers of saints . . .

> And every creature which is in heaven, and on the earth,
> and under the earth, and such as are in the sea, and all
> that are in them, heard I saying, Blessing, and honour,
> and glory, and power, be unto him that sitteth upon the
> throne, and unto the Lamb for ever and ever.
>
> Revelation 5:1-8, 13

Have you ever thought about the actual ownership of
the planet Earth? It has always been a valuable property, and through the centuries men and nations have
tried to stake out their diverse claims to it. I invite you to
spend a little time with me in the fifth chapter of the
Revelation as we seek to answer the question, "Who
really owns this world, after all?" and as we consider
some implications of that answer.

John is still gazing through the door standing open in
heaven. He is being shown important scenes and mighty
deeds—cosmic events that will affect the entire created
universe.

John sees an important document in the right hand of
the One sitting on the throne: a scroll securely sealed
with seven seals. Then he hears the voice of a "mighty
angel" asking the entire universe, "Who is worthy to
open the book, and to loose the seals thereof?"

Bible commentators have had differing opinions
about this written, sealed document. Some have said it
might be the Old Testament. Others have countered that
it probably was the New Testament. Some scholars have
held that it was God's book of judgment. One imagina-
tive person suggested that it was "the statement of
God's hidden purposes."

A number of other godly students of the Word hold
that this scroll was the actual title deed to the created
earth. That is what I believe, too, and I think there is
scriptural reason for such an opinion.

Our inclination is to say that God owns and controls all things, but Satan and his hosts have long challenged God's right and God's control. Remember the temptation of our Lord and the daring proposition of the devil:

> Again, the devil taketh him up into an exceeding high mountain, and sheweth him all the kingdoms of the world, and the glory of them; And saith unto him, All these things will I give thee, if thou wilt fall down and worship me.
>
> Then saith Jesus unto him, Get thee hence, Satan: for it is written, Thou shalt worship the Lord thy God, and him only shalt thou serve. (Matthew 4:8-10)

We note that our Lord did not challenge the implied claim Satan made concerning the kingdoms of this world. His reply to the devil was: "I will not worship you. God alone deserves worship!"

## Satan, the usurper

So, Satan has made his claims, and in many ways he has succeeded in exercising control through the centuries, even though he certainly could not produce a title deed.

We need at this point to review the scriptural background of creation and the fall of man. When God created Adam, He said in effect: "I am giving you the title to this good earth, and I am giving you dominion over it and over the creatures on the earth, the fish in the seas and the birds in the air. There are a few rules you must observe, however. For one, you must not eat of the tree of the knowledge of good and evil!"

Tempted by Satan, Adam and Eve ate the forbidden fruit. Their disobedience introduced death to the human race. The ground was cursed, and sinning mankind forfeited ready fellowship with God. In effect, the creator God took back the title deed He had given our first parents.

We seldom consider it just this way, but when Adam and Eve succumbed to Satan's proposition in the Garden of Eden, they allowed him to become a squatter—an alien usurper of dominion throughout the earth, even though he did not hold the title deed.

How could the earth ever be redeemed from this encroacher and mankind restored? There was only one way—a seemingly impossible way. There must of necessity be a Second Adam. He must be able to meet the tempter and best him. Moreover, because death had come through sin, the Second Adam would have to taste death and emerge its victor. Only in such a way could mankind win back all that had been lost in the Garden.

## Who owns this world?

Who owns the world? Ever since God's right to His creation has been challenged by the forces of Satan and the fantasies of sinful men and women, our world has had its succession of dark and dreadful rulers.

The intellectuals—those wise in this world's wisdom—would have us believe that only they have the capacity for dominance and rulership. It is just as well that they have not usually prevailed. It would be grim, indeed, if the course of this world were shaped by the thinkers. Most of them seem miserable and unhappy. Ecclesiastes is the soliloquy of perhaps the world's wisest man—a great thinker. He becomes more gloomy as he goes along. Finally, after "[giving] [him]self to seek and search out by wisdom concerning all things that are done under heaven" (1:13), he comes to this morbid exclamation:

"Vanity of vanities, saith the preacher; all is vanity" (12:8).

Another group who insist they are capable of wielding world power are the blue-collar workers—those who toil for a living. Their slogan has been a popular one in this century: "Workers of the world, arise! You have nothing to lose but your chains!" But we have discovered to our sorrow that worker power is no better than the moral level of the workers; once in authority, they can be both cruel and tyrannical.

Probably I should also mention the scientists in this discussion of world force and technology. Some think the scientists are qualified to exercise world oversight. But what do we see? On the one hand, we see learned men and women able to heal and save lives. On the other hand, we see men and women inventing new ways to destroy the greatest number of people in the shortest space of time. The scientists have not demonstrated their ability to bring good government to our world.

Then, there are the claims of the various human races. From the Pharaohs of ancient Egypt to the cataclysmic, racial-inspired wars of this century, we have seen the devastation heaped upon mankind as one or another race sought to assert its superiority.

When Jesus Christ was on earth, He warned His followers in plain language that wars and rumors of war would continue right up to the time of His return. We are reluctant witnesses to the truth of His words. In the dark days of World War II, when the outcome of that conflagration was still in the balance, this was my Christian counsel to my congregation:

"No matter how things look to us now, sin and murder and violence cannot win at last. Righteousness and godliness cannot fail at last. Prophecy must be fulfilled. We will see the day when Germany's mouthing maniac will go down like a rotten tree felled on the hillside. Let us stay by our faith. It is still right to be good, and it is still wrong to follow evil. God must still rule His world, and Christ must still be the acclaimed King throughout the universe." I believed it then. I believe it yet.

## Communism is no different

Since those days, communism has reared its head. Millions have feared that it was only a matter of time until the world would be under Communist ideology and control. Silly, frightened people declared they would "rather be Red than dead." But communism cannot prevail, and I will tell you why. It has nothing to do with politics or economics or public ownership of property.

Communism cannot prevail because it begins with materialism. It teaches that there is no God and no Christ, no heaven and no hell. It declares that mankind has no soul and that prayer to God is nonsense. Communism is a negation of everything good and pure, everything divine and holy. It cannot prevail because our God in heaven has His plan and program for creation. There is no human being and no human philosophy or force able to wrest dominion from our living God.

When John looked through the open door into heaven, he saw this significant title deed in the hands of God, who sat on the throne. The great angel's voice went throughout creation as if in challenge to Satan and every created being: "Who is worthy to break the seals and open the scroll?"

And what was the response? No one in heaven or on earth or under the earth was qualified to open the scroll or to look inside it. All of this uncertainty was too much for the sensitive, tender John. I have often thought of John's great heart of love and concern and have decided that I would rather have a heart like his than all the knowledge this world holds.

We must not forget that John was still human and still much a part of the earth scene when he received this vision. He was not yet glorified, not yet perfected. In his own being, John treasured the prospect of God's control and ownership of our lost planet. John knew from observation and experience the telltale signs of having the wrong person in political charge. He was isolated on Patmos because of his Christian testimony.

I think John carried the grief of the human race in his heart. That was why God chose him to receive the Revelation. God always blesses the men and women who have concern enough in their hearts to bring tears of love and compassion to their eyes. We have many ways of teaching the Bible and theology—and I believe in them. But I must insist that the Spirit of God will reveal some of the secrets of God only to those who know what it means to have a broken heart for Jesus' sake and on behalf of lost humanity.

So, one of the elders said to John, "Do not weep! See, the Lion of the tribe of Judah, the Root of David, has triumphed. He is able to open the scroll and its seven seals." John knew what a lion was like, and he turned in expectation. But the One he saw was not a lion but a Lamb—the Lamb of God!

> And I beheld, and, lo, in the midst of the throne and of the four beasts, and in the midst of the elders, stood a Lamb as it had been slain, having seven horns and seven

> eyes, which are the seven Spirits of God sent forth into all the earth. And he came and took the book out of the right hand of him that sat upon the throne . . .
>
> And every creature which is in heaven, and on the earth, and under the earth, and such as are in the sea, and all that are in them, heard I saying, Blessing, and honour, and glory, and power, be unto him that sitteth upon the throne, and unto the Lamb for ever and ever (5:6-7, 13).

Now, I want to look back with you to this scene in which the Lion and the Lamb are mentioned. The association seems odd to us. We wonder how it could be. John was told that the Lion of the tribe of Judah was the conqueror, but when he turned, he saw not the fearful and powerful Lion but the wondrous Lamb of God, the risen and eternal Christ.

Let us fully understand this truth. On earth, the lion is stronger than the lamb. But in the kingdom of God and before the throne of God, the Lamb is stronger, and He is Victor! God's ways and ours are not the same. When John turned, he saw Christ, the Lion, but in truth he saw Him as the Lamb. Unless we know Jesus Christ as both Lamb, our Redeemer, and Lion, our strength to live for Him day by day, we are not Christians in the right sense of the word. In the kingdoms of earth, the spirit of the lion dominates; in the kingdom of God, the Lamb rules. For this reason the world's redemption is not in mankind's hands.

If you get nothing else from this chapter, it is essential that you understand and retain this truth: the world's redemption is not in mankind's hands. I cannot tell you how glad I am that there is at least one thing that we humans cannot bungle. The plan of salvation is God's plan. The power in redemption is God's power. Only the

Lamb of God could die in our place. This is God's way of doing things, not ours.

## Not the strong fists, but the nail-pierced hands

God redeemed lost mankind not by the strong fists of Jesus but by His nail-pierced hands. We do not sing about the power of the clenched fist; we sing with thanksgiving that we "shall know Him by the print of the nails in His hands." This gospel of Jesus Christ is unique. There is nothing within it that brings glory or credit to our human means or methods. Our redemption was not by muscle, but by love. It was not wrought by vengeance, but by forgiveness. It was not by sword, but by sacrifice.

We are Christians because Jesus destroyed His enemies by dying for them. He conquered death by letting death conquer Him, and then He turned death inside out as He burst forth from the tomb as Victor! This whole work of redemption had to be accomplished in the way things are done in heaven. That is why I say that as Christians, we have learned that whatever Christ the Lion will do in bringing the world into submission, He will do because of what He has already done as the Lamb of God.

The scenes in this part of the Revelation are not provincial. By that, I mean they do not deal just with Israel or just with the church. If you please, they do not even deal just with our planet. Almighty God is dealing with all of His vast, created universe. The unlimited search for One worthy to claim the title deed to creation was indeed a universal search. Not just earth, but our whole universe awaits the consummation. Who is worthy? Who is able? Who is the Conqueror?

In this world, ruined and turned upside down by sin, God had a better way, whether or not people will accept it. Jesus invaded our world as God's Christ. He conquered by the shedding of His own blood. For the first and only time, victory was fashioned in such an unorthodox way. Now the Lamb, who is also the Lion, stands in the midst of that heavenly throne.

God is saying to all the universe: "The time has come for you to understand that I am God. Earthlings must give up their sinful, distorted ideas of strength and power and dominion. Only this victorious Lamb is worthy to claim the title deed to the created universe and to open the seals that are holding back My judgments."

## Not a pleasant subject

Judgment and God's wrath are not pleasant subjects. I know people who turn away, saying with finality: "I do not even want to think about judgment. I will not discuss it!"

We do not fully understand all of God's purposes in preserving for our time and generation this Revelation. But we do know that this world's cup of iniquity is filling up. We know there are warnings in this book that continually urge us to be watchful, thoughtful believers.

I am convinced of this: we Christians in our minds and hearts must always be correcting what we hear and see against the truth of heaven. Otherwise, we will be carried away by the world and its distorted human ways and values. How did the nations of earth come to be what they are? By tooth and claw—the law of the jungle. The questions of justice, right and righteousness—these scarcely come up at all. I confess that I am afraid for this sinful and violent society. I am afraid, indeed, for the millions and millions of men and women who defy God, who hate Jesus Christ and who are willing dupes of Satan.

When the cup of iniquity is full, God cannot withhold judgment any longer. The Bible gives us an ample, frightening preview of the tribulation that will come upon the earth. In our Christian circles the question often is asked, "Will the church go through the tribulation? Will the church be raptured out of this world before the great tribulation begins?"

There are differences of opinion and a variety of interpretations concerning the sequence of events when Christ returns. I am not among those who claim to have all the answers. I know there is a time of great tribulation coming upon our world. Whether the church of Jesus Christ shall escape all of that judgment and suffering is not clear. I fear the church will suffer trial and tribulation. At the same time, I have a great hope that it will not!

I shall not argue about it. I will not debate the matter. For myself, I know I do not want to be on this earth when that worst of all time comes—when God rises up and shakes the earth and the nations so that those things that cannot be shaken may remain.

John has described the heavenly scene in which the angels of God are being prepared for the judgments that must come upon this planet. I can only wonder how much longer the holy patience of God can stand by in grace and mercy.

The Lamb of God is the Conqueror. John saw that confirmed at the throne of God in heaven. The day may be near when the Conqueror goes forth to establish His righteous rule in all the earth!

# 7.

## The Beginning of Judgments in Revelation: "The Four Horsemen!"

And I saw when the Lamb opened one of the seals, and I heard, as it were the noise of thunder, one of the four beasts saying, Come and see. And I saw, and behold a white horse: and he that sat on him had a bow; and a crown was given unto him: and he went forth conquering, and to conquer. And when he had opened the second seal, I heard the second beast say, Come and see. And there went out another horse that was red: and power was given to him that sat thereon to take peace from the earth, and that they should kill one another: and there was given unto him a great sword. And when he had opened the third seal, I heard the third beast say, Come and see. And I beheld, and lo a black horse; and he that sat on him had a pair of balances in his hand. And I heard a voice in the midst of the four beasts say, A measure of wheat for a penny, and three measures of barley for a penny; and see thou hurt not the oil and the wine. And when he had opened the fourth seal, I heard the voice of the fourth beast say, Come and see. And I looked, and behold a pale horse: and his name that sat on him was Death, and Hell followed with him. And power was given unto them over the fourth part of the earth, to kill with sword, and with hunger, and with death, and with the beasts of the earth . . .

And the kings of the earth, and the great men, and the rich men, and the chief captains, and the mighty men, and every bondman, and every free man, hid themselves in the dens and in the rocks of the mountains; And said to the mountains and rocks, Fall on us, and hide us from the face of him that sitteth on the throne, and from the wrath of the Lamb: For the great day of his wrath is come; and who shall be able to stand?

                                        Revelation 6:1-8, 15-17

In all of secular and sacred literature, perhaps no other cast of characters has evoked the kind of universal discussion and conjecture accorded the four horsemen of the Apocalypse. Because the Scriptures present the dramatic appearances of these four horsemen against the vivid backdrop of God's wrath and judgment, most humans have ultimately reacted with incredulity:

"The judgments cannot be real. The famine, the plagues cannot be real. Our world is too good; men and women are too good to deserve the judgment of God. Forget the whole idea. Think nothing more about it. Such a judgment will never happen."

Even in the worst of its dark and fearsome times, the human race has never given up hoping for "something better" to happen in the future. The poet sensed that yearning when he pointed out the often quoted truth: "Hope springs eternal in the human breast."

Men and women have never given up their fond hope that the earth next year—or perhaps the year after that—

will be a better place in which to live! In spite of war and rumors of war, men and women never abandon their unfounded hope that lasting peace is about to become reality.

Politicians have learned that they can garner votes if they will fan the hopes of constituents that this world actually can be made a place of universal health. I listen to the campaign speeches of the candidates for public office. Their appeal is based largely on their promise to solve all economic and social problems. Then, after four years, we discover that our "paradise" has not happened.

Even in the realm of the church and religion, we hear expressions of hope that religious unity can be achieved. These churchmen fondly hope that the social problems will go away once everyone is worshiping in one large church. The extra and unnecessary church properties can become playgrounds and recreational centers for the well-being of the deprived children in our communities.

## A sharp contrast

I have cited these often expressed hopes because they are in sharp contrast to what we see concerning the four horsemen of the Revelation. In doing so, I abandon any lingering hope of popularity, for what I see is counter to our natural desires for peace, tranquility and unity. But I am committed to the truth, whether or not it is popular. And the truth is that all of these human hopes we have reviewed are vain hopes. This world is not going to get better under human government.

Likely you know someone who is terminally ill. If you learn of even slight improvement in the person's condition, you are glad. But in your heart of hearts you know the change is temporary. Death is only a matter of time.

In the case of our world, it received a mortal wound some six millenniums ago. A preacher here and there may say, "I think I see a little improvement." But this is a sinful and rebellious world. Its long list of ailments and ills will not fade away. The longer-term prognosis has not changed. The world is not going to heal itself.

In this section of the Revelation there is a noticeable sense of heavenly excitement. There is intense interest, eager expectation and ecstatic worship as the Lion of the tribe of Judah steps forward. The One who has conquered as the Lamb of God steps forward to receive the seven-sealed scroll, a written document that is best understood as the accredited title deed to this earth.

There is a burst of acclamation around the heavenly throne as every voice sings:

> Worthy is the Lamb that was slain
> to receive power, and riches, and wisdom, and strength,
> and honour, and glory, and blessing! (5:12)

Then John heard the most unusual sound of all: the voices of "every creature which is in heaven, and on the earth, and under the earth, and such as are in the sea, and all that are in them, heard I saying, Blessing, and honour, and glory, and power, be unto him that sitteth upon the throne, and unto the Lamb for ever and ever" (5:13).

And he adds, "The four beasts said, Amen, and the four and twenty elders fell down and worshipped."

## The mysterious seals

The sixth chapter begins abruptly with the opening of the mysterious seals having to do with the title deed to this earth. John tells us he watched as the Lamb opened the first of the seven seals. At once, one of the living creatures said in a voice like thunder, "Come!" This is the long-awaited signal to the four horsemen that the hour has come for them to gallop forth on their missions of judgment.

When Jesus was on earth 2,000 years ago, He told His hearers that the "day of the Lord" was coming. He said no one except the Father in heaven knew the day or the hour. It is our understanding that God's patience and His time of grace will endure until the world's cup of iniquity overflows. According to the Scriptures, patience—the ability to wait—is one of the fruits of the Holy Spirit. The human, natural part of us does not like to wait for anything. But the great God Almighty, who has all of eternity to accomplish His purposes, can afford to wait. In our creature impatience we are prone to cry out, "O God, how long? How long?" And God replies, in effect, "Why are you in such a hurry? We have an eternity stretching before us. Why get excited and irritated?"

Apparently the four symbolic steeds have been prepared and waiting for this summons. In equestrian language, they were "champing at the bit." But they had to wait for events on earth and in heaven to run their course before they could go into action. During that long wait, generations of Christian believers have lived with the expectation of the Lord's return to earth. Not all of them were patient. Not all of them had the ability to wait. Some began to say, "He will not return!"

Now, John continues with the narration of what he saw:

> And I saw, and behold a white horse: and he that sat on him had a bow; and a crown was given unto him: and he went forth conquering, and to conquer.

Some have asked, "Could this rider on the white horse be Christ Jesus?" The answer is a definite "No." Within this context, he could not possibly be Christ Jesus, for it is Christ Jesus—the Lamb—who has broken the seal that frees the horseman to go forth. Inasmuch as all four of these horsemen are connected with judgment, we must identify the rider of the white horse as one who will prove to be a deceiver of mankind and a curse. Most scholars, indeed, look upon him as the antichrist.

## An antichrist will come

In other places in the Bible such an antichrist is announced (see, for example, 1 John 4:3). Destined to appear at some future time of world crisis, he will be a deceiver, conquering by lies and duplicity (see Daniel 8:23-25). He will be known as "the man of lawlessness" (2 Thessalonians 2:3), and in the course of his dominance over mankind he will ultimately exalt himself as God.

There is reason to expect that those who are pressing for one great world church will welcome and cooperate with the antichrist when he appears. Indeed, he will be favorable to religious interests—for a while! When he sees the church wishing to move in a certain direction, he will say to the membership, "The key to this objective is to be tolerant—you must love everybody! "Then, while men and women are busy loving everybody and being tolerant, those religious leaders will take over and put their stamp upon the world.

We have had illustrations of this in our own time. While men and women are intent on brotherhood, love and unity, teachers are busy telling our young people in high school and college that God did not create the heavens and the earth, that Adam and Eve did not really exist, that Christ's resurrection from the dead is a myth.

Yes, an antichrist is destined to enter the world scene. His control, as I said, will be through duplicity and delusion. He will appear to be an amiable person, able to head up and harness all the divergent political, economic and religious forces. Ultimately he will turn out to be the embodiment of everything that is contrary to our Lord Jesus Christ. When he comes, he will talk much about peace and prosperity. But during his regime, war will come. That armed conflict is the signal for the second horse to appear.

## The fiery red horse of war

This second horseman "was given power to take peace from the earth and to make men slay each other." The pacifists and the optimists will argue against this portrait of future war. But the antichrist's campaign of religious brotherhood and international peace will be short lived. Satan is the world's greatest counterfeiter, and he is behind the duplicity of this counterfeit Christ!

Suppose some person or force in our world could proclaim that tomorrow morning all wars and all conflict would cease, that all soldiers, sailors and airmen would go home, that all military bases would be permanently closed, that the entrenched military industrial complex would be no more. The proclamation would call for complete world disarmament; no nation would be permitted to go to war ever again.

What would follow in the wake of such a worldwide edict? Everyone knows the answer. The worst economic depression in the history of mankind would quickly develop. Where would the world's governments find jobs for the millions of people who are currently a part of the defense and military establishments? Or for the added millions whose jobs are in the civilian support networks for the nations' armies?

The antichrist has promised prosperity. To achieve it, he will resort to war and conquest. John was told that this second horseman was given power to take peace from the world and "to make men slay each other." When this horseman rides forth, any temporary treaties of peace and cooperation will be disregarded. We are reminded of what the apostle Paul predicted would happen as the "day of the Lord" came: "For when they shall say, Peace and safety; then sudden destruction cometh upon them, as travail upon a woman with child; and they shall not escape" (1 Thessalonians 5:3). The symbolism is plain. This rider with the character of war has a great sword given to him—a sword that surely represents mankind's capacity to wage international warfare.

## Aftermath of war: famine and death

When the third living creature issues his thunderous invitation to "Come!" a black horse charges into the world arena. The description of the rider of the black horse is clearly famine.

It should not be surprising to us that famine and hunger will follow quickly on the heels of war and the disdain for human life. We have seen it happen too many times. When vast sections of humanity are affected by war, the dislocated masses begin to starve.

Inevitably, the fourth horseman rides abroad on his pale steed. There is no mistaking his identity. Death is his name. John records that the forces of Hades—hell—come along closely behind him. To the power of death by sword is added the power of death by famine, plague and wild beast.

We really have no idea what world conditions will be in that day. Biological warfare will be added to the destructive elements already in use. Plague is the name for it: diseases that quickly break forth from the rotting corpses that no one has time to mourn or to bury. And when these four seals have been broken by the victorious Lamb, judgment and tribulation, pain and death will overflow our earth.

You may be accusing me of extreme pessimism. So be it. But I must agree with what John foretells, for it is a part of the Bible, and the Bible is wholly true. We live in the midst of an ungodly society—a world that rebels against our God and His Christ. I do not find anything in the Word of God to encourage this generation in its present godless lifestyle. It resolves no problems for men and women to say to each other, "Cheer up! Things will get better!" All is not well. Things will not get better while the horses of the apocalypse are pawing the ground and champing at the bit, awaiting the signal to gallop forth.

As I close this chapter, I want to tie in the loosing of these four horsemen with John's vision of the souls of the martyrs beneath the altar (6:9-11) when the fifth seal is broken. John says he immediately heard the "loud voice" of these souls "under the altar." Their appeal: "How long, O Lord, holy and true, dost thou not judge and avenge our blood on them that dwell on the earth?"

I think it is beautiful how God answers them as a mother might comfort her children. John says, "Then each of them was given a white robe, and they were told to wait a little longer, until the number of their fellow servants and brothers who were to be killed as they had been was completed." It is as if God says, "Hush, My

dear children. Do not be impatient. We are waiting a little longer until the souls of the other faithful martyrs are
gathered in. They are giving up their lives even as you
have given yours. Meanwhile, here are shining robes to
wear until the time is ripe!"

## The martyrs' place

I doubt that the souls of these martyrs are in some seg-
regated part of the heavenly realm. John hears their
appeal at his time because of the judgments about to
take place. Further, I do not interpret their call as blood-
thirsty. My mind goes out to the great roll call of the
faithful, holy men and women slain in every century for
their testimony of love for Jesus Christ. I think, for
example, of Stephen, stoned to death by infuriated Jews
whom he had charged with the betrayal and murder of
God's Righteous One. But as he died, Stephen prayed,
"Lord, lay not this sin to their charge" (Acts 7:60).

The breaking of that fifth seal seems to indicate that
the martyrs had been told earlier that God would never
forget their love, loyalty and obedience to Jesus Christ.
Vengeance, the Bible admonishes us, does not belong to
us (Romans 12:19). As Christians, we willingly live for
God in a hostile world because God has already whis-
pered to us, "Be patient; be kind! Any vengeance that is
necessary will be My holy vengeance. I will repay!"

Surely we do not think often enough of this great
company of overcomers who have told their tormentors
on this earth: "Do what you want with us. We will love
and honor our Savior, Jesus Christ—to the death if necessary!" When our godless society martyrs a saint of
God, it is a frightful act of injustice—an unspeakable act
of fallen man's deepest depravity.

History has a way of mixing up the accounts and coloring the tales men tell, but God in heaven keeps faithful records. He alone knows every detail about the faith and courage of every person who has laid down his or her human life for the Savior, Jesus Christ. So this cry as the martyrs wait is not a cry for blood. It is a cry for the day and hour when God's judgment upon all of mankind's sin and unholiness will come.

We are right in believing that God has a plan and that it is both fixed and eternal. I do not dismiss the Revelation. I do not dismiss the fact that God is going to deal with Satan—that deadly, cunning usurper of God's created earth. I do not try to explain away these coming judgments. I trust the prediction of the Scriptures that these four horsemen of judgment and death will ride out over the nations of this earth. I take this view because I know that men and women once created in the image of God, now continue to violate His holy laws, hour after hour, year after year.

## One of my burdens

I share with you one of my great burdens concerning our present generation. Our wisest and most brilliant people have played with the secrets of God Almighty, the Creator. I do not know how we can justify it. For the first time in the history of the world, we have released the secret of the composition of matter. Sinful men have entered into that holy place where life begins. We have glorified our test tubes, our microscopes, our instruments of technology, prying into the secrets of creation and life-secrets that have always belonged only to God.

The problems of death and destruction we have not solved. Nuclear destruction is out of the bottle—and becoming more menacing by the year. The common people do not really know the extent to which their leaders have mortgaged their futures. So they repress their fears and doubts by seeking pleasure and living selfishly, intent only on themselves. Someone has described their lifestyle as "pampered opulence." While the world is falling apart, they are spending billions on fun and on pleasure and on what they call excitement.

We may have differing opinions about the symbols and details of prophetic warnings, but God's truth is here. We cannot get around it. Into history, into our world, the horsemen of the Apocalypse will come riding forth in God's time. Dare we imagine we can live in pampered opulence—not even remembering to pray for this dying world—and still believe we will be ready for that hour when our Lord will call His people home?

As a minister of God's Word, I add my caution to every caution and warning God has given us. If we are wasting our time and money and energy in foolish play, it will be tragic for us in that awful, coming hour.

I pray for myself. I pray that I may be more detached from this world and from its evils and its selfish systems. I pray that I may recognize that soft, silky, deceptive voice that is opposed to our Lord Jesus Christ. I pray that I will be able to stand with the overcomers, even if it means that everyone around me is an enemy, even if it means martyrdom.

Do you feel that way about these important issues? I hope you do!

# 8.

# The Overcomers in Revelation: "Out of the Great Tribulation!"

And after these things I saw four angels standing on the four corners of the earth, holding the four winds of the earth, that the wind should not blow on the earth, nor on the sea, nor on any tree. And I saw another angel ascending from the east, having the seal of the living God: and he cried with a loud voice to the four angels, to whom it was given to hurt the earth and the sea, saying, Hurt not the earth, neither the sea, nor the trees, till we have sealed the servants of our God in their foreheads. And I heard the number of them which were sealed: and there were sealed an hundred and forty and four thousand of all the tribes of the children of Israel . . .

After this I beheld, and, lo, a great multitude, which no man could number, of all nations, and kindreds, and people, and tongues, stood before the throne, and before the Lamb, clothed with white robes, and palms in their hands . . .

And one of the elders answered, saying unto me, What are these which are arrayed in white robes? and whence came they?

And I said unto him, Sir, thou knowest. And he said to me, These are they which came out of great tribulation, and have washed their robes, and made them white in the blood of the Lamb.

Revelation 7:1-4, 9, 13-14

The most tragic and unavailing prayer meeting in the history of the world is described for us in the sixth chapter of the Revelation. In the seventh, the apostle John reports the greatest ever assembly of the redeemed for praise and worship. Both events follow the unloosing in heaven of the mysterious sixth seal by the worthy, victorious Lamb of God.

All varieties of prayer—cries and groans, shouts and demands, moans and whispers—will be heard in that coming day of the Lord when the forces of judgment are released, when the stars begin to fall, when even the mountains and the islands will be removed from their places. But by then the prayers and cries of sinful men and women will be too little and too late. All of the great men of the earth, all of the important people, all who have mistakenly put their trust and their hope in purely human abilities will join those crying out in guilt. They will call on the crumbling rocks and mountains to fall on them to hide them from the wrath of God.

John foresees a great earthquake. The sun turns black. The moon becomes blood-red. Stars fall to the earth. The sky recedes like a scroll and every mountain and island is dislocated.

I am among those who believe that the judgments of God are certain. God is indeed going to shake the earth as it has never been shaken before. I do not know the day when these events will happen. I do not know the hour. That is confidential information known only to my heavenly Father. Jesus himself told us not to waste our

efforts speculating on "the times and dates the Father
has set by his own authority" (Acts 1:7).

As these seals are opened, our earth experiences heavenly phenomena that rock and shake the planet. The
earthquake that will take place will be devastating in its
destruction.

I have never experienced an earthquake. Those who
have say the greatest terror is the sudden and extreme
loss of confidence in the earth itself. Psychologists con-
firm that such an experience can leave the human system in deep, long-term shock. Until the moment of the
quake, the earth has been a stable, supportive friend.
Suddenly it is that no longer! Floors, walls, ceilings are
no longer fixed and certain. Everything—including the
earth itself—seems to recede. The shaking, the rocking,
the rumbling—all of these phenomena tell the finite
human being that his or her life-long confidence in the
terra firma has been a misplaced trust.

## Far beyond man's tinkering

We have become complacent about scientific technology
and space exploration. We even joke about all the
American and Russian metal orbiting the earth and
speculate that some sort of a space traffic cop will soon
be necessary to keep the traffic lanes open!

But these things that mankind and nations do as a
result of their science and technology are as nothing
compared with the shaking that will occur after the
opening of the sixth seal. At least up until this time, our
discoveries and experiments in space have not affected
the sun and the stars. But God intends to take things out
of human hands and human control. In an instant he
will convince mankind and nations of the fatal mistake

they have made—the mistake of forgetting God and elevating human ability and performance in the place of God.

What God has to say to us in Revelation 6 is a sobering preview. Even for us who are Christians it is difficult to realize the extent of this divine judgment upon our earth. In a word, all inhabitants left on the earth—"kings of the earth, the princes, the generals, the rich, the mighty, and every slave and every free man"—will be reduced to helplessness and stark fear. Regardless of status, rank or position, men and women will seek a hiding place from God's wrath: "They called to the mountains and the rocks, 'Fall on us and hide us from the face of him who sits on the throne and from the wrath of the Lamb! For the great day of their wrath has come, and who can stand?'"

God is obliged to bring this event to pass. Proud and sinful humans, in their blasphemous pursuits, have long profaned the name of Jesus, the heavenly Lamb. They have imagined themselves smart enough, able enough, strong enough to be successful in their rebellion against the suffering Savior.

## The outraged Lamb

People might have imagined that the Lion of Judah had a measure of power and strength. But suddenly God reveals His wrath through the outraged Lamb. It is the Lamb who has been found worthy! It is the Lamb who is the Victor, the Overcomer! It is the Lamb of God, God's eternal Son, into whose hands the Father has committed all justice and judgment!

What a great responsibility God has laid upon us preachers of His gospel and teachers of His Word. In that future day when God's wrath is poured out, how are we going to answer? How am I going to answer? I fear there is much we are doing in the name of the Christian church that is wood, hay and stubble destined to be burned up in God's refining fire. A day is coming when I and my fellow ministers must give account of our stewardship:

- What kind of a gospel did we preach?
- Did we make it plain that men and women who are apart from Christ Jesus are lost?
- Did we counsel them to repent and believe?
- Did we tell them of the regenerating power of the Holy Spirit?
- Did we warn them of the wrath of the Lamb—the crucified, resurrected, outraged Lamb of God?
- With that kind of accounting yet to come, the question John hears from the human objects of God's wrath is especially significant: "Who shall be able to stand?" (6:17). Who indeed?

I reflect back to the evangelistic preaching throughout the cities of America by the famous Billy Sunday. Billy Sunday had many critics, but he plowed a deep furrow for God in the hearts and minds of sinful, lost men and women. In his meetings, Billy frequently used a song entitled, "The Great Judgment Morning." We no longer hear it in our churches, and that does not speak well for our theology. Perhaps we have gone soft on judgment and accountability. Perhaps we have gone soft on our responsibility to the lost.

But Billy Sunday told people they were destined to face the judgment of God. "The Great Judgment Morning" sung in his meetings told of one person's dream of judgment morning when the great man's greatness was no more and the rich man's wealth had disappeared. All that remained was the haunting question, "Who shall be able to stand?"

I thank God that there is an answer to that question. Those who have quit their sin, who are clothed in Jesus Christ's righteousness—they will be able to stand! The reason the kings and the great men, the slaves and the free men are in such terror is because they love their sin more than anything else. Sin is just too dear to give up.

## What price earth's baubles?

I heard of a Kansas farm family endangered by a sudden, descending tornado. The mother quickly herded all her children into the safety of a storm cellar below ground level. But then, in a moment, she disappeared—dashing up into the house to save a little knickknack that she treasured for sentimental value. Before she could return to safety, that roaring, twisting funnel of wind and fury tore the house to pieces. In minutes it passed and was gone. The children found their mother in the rubble, bleeding, unconscious and dying.

Who will be able to stand? Those who have given up their worthless earthly trinkets, those who have quit loving this world above all else, those who have abandoned hope that anything down here is of permanence and value, those who have come to hate their own sin as God hates it—they will be able to stand!

The Revelation refers often to the over comers in that future day. They will be able to stand then because they have stood firm here and now against every effort of the devil to discourage and tempt and deceive them.

## The scene changes

We leave the scene of earthly judgment as we move into chapter seven of the Revelation. There John describes a scene of joyful praise and worship unmatched in all of history. John sees "a great multitude, which no man could number, of all nations, and kindreds, and people, and tongues, stood before the throne, and before the Lamb." John goes on to say, "They were clothed with white robes, and palms in their hands." And their song was an anthem of praise to God and the Lamb:

> Blessing, and glory,
> and wisdom, and thanksgiving, and honour,
> and power, and might,
> be unto our God for ever and ever.
> Amen!

While God's judgments are visited upon the earth, the overcomers seem to be spared to join the vast throng of the redeemed and glorified saints in heaven.

The chapter begins with an amazing description of four strong angels holding back the four winds of the earth—winds of judgment and distress. As they wait, another angel calls out to them, "Hurt not the earth, neither the sea, nor the trees, till we have sealed the servants of our God in their foreheads" (7:3).

## The seal was used in the Old Testament

God's use of a seal on His faithful people is not unprecedented. In Ezekiel 9, God instructed the "man clothed with linen" to "go through the midst of the city, through the midst of Jerusalem, and set a mark upon the foreheads of the men that sigh and that cry for all the abominations that be done in the midst thereof" (9:4). Then, to the six men with the "slaughter weapons" God commands: "Go ye after him through the city, and smite: let not your eye spare, neither have ye pity: Slay utterly old and young, both maids, and little children, and women: but come not near any man upon whom is the mark; and begin at my sanctuary" (9:5-6). Ezekiel adds, "Then they began at the ancient men which were before the house."

Next John describes God's sealing of the 144,000 "from all the tribes of the children of Israel," 12,000 from each of the 12 tribes (Revelation 7:4-8). I do not in the least agree with the numerous cults and far-out religious groups who insist that only they themselves will be sealed as God's elect. Many of us in the evangelical tradition are convinced the Bible predicts a glorious, eternal future for a believing "remnant" within Jewry. How does the present state of Israel fit into the picture? With all my heart I believe that God did not lie to Abraham! There will be a remnant of believing Jews, restored from north, south, east and west, who will occupy the land God gave to Abraham, Isaac and Jacob.

But I press on now to John's portrayal of the great host of redeemed saints praising and worshiping God around the heavenly throne. This is certainly one of the most amazing passages in the entire Bible—and, in my opinion, one of the most beautiful.

John succeeds as well as anyone could in describing the great multitude from every tribe and nation and language on earth. All are clothed in white robes. All hold palm branches signifying victory. And they are crying out:

> Salvation to our God
> which sitteth upon the throne,
> and unto the Lamb.

Then they join the host of angels around the throne, together with the elders and the living creatures in a song of praise and adoration:

> Amen:
> Blessing, and glory, and
> wisdom, and thanksgiving, and honour,
> and power, and might, be unto our God
> for ever and ever.
> Amen.

I have tried to think what my own emotions and delight would be if I, like John, could have been a witness to this heavenly outpouring of worship and praise. John must have been ecstatic. He must have been speechless with reverence and awe.

## John is asked a question

Suddenly, one of the heavenly elders asked John a question. "What are these which are arrayed in white robes? and whence came they?" John was an example of true Christian humility. This apostle who had spent three years in the company of Jesus, who had devoted a lifetime to teaching and pastoral ministry, did not fish around for some expansive answer that would reveal his expertise and knowledge. He simply shook his head and replied, "Sir, you know." This was the true John. How I would like to say to him, "John, what a wonderful and humble Christian brother you are! How I would like to be more like you!"

So the elder tells John: "These are they which came out of great tribulation, and have washed their robes, and made them white in the blood of the Lamb.

Therefore, are they before the throne of God, and serve him day and night in his temple: and he that sitteth on the throne shall dwell among them. They shall hunger no more, neither thirst any more; neither shall the sun light on them, nor any heat. For the Lamb which is in the midst of the throne shall feed them, and shall lead them unto living fountains of waters: and God shall wipe away all tears from their eyes."

Where in all this world could we turn to find anything as beautiful, as powerful, as overwhelming as this description of the overcoming saints of God in heaven? I recommend that we stop reading the shallow, worldly stuff of our day—material that is not doing our souls any good. We should concentrate more of our time and attention on where we are going for eternity.

The assembly of saints described in this chapter of the Revelation is a specific company. I know that. But all of these things that God is doing for them, He has promised to do for all of His believing children. We should not be engaged in useless argument about who may be called upon to suffer and even give their lives for the testimony of Jesus Christ. Concerning this numberless multitude John is told that they have come through the great tribulation. On earth their witness and stand for Christ cost them everything, but in heaven they are the overcomers around the royal throne.

We are 20th century Christians. Some of us are Christians only because it is convenient and pleasant and because it is not costing us anything. But here is the truth, whether we like it or not: the average evangelical Christian who claims to be born again and have eternal life is not doing as much to propagate his or her faith as the busy adherents of the cults handing out their papers on the street corners and visiting from house to house.

We are not willing to take the spit and the contempt and the abuses those cultists take as they knock on doors and try to persuade everyone to follow them in their mistaken beliefs. The cultists can teach us much about zeal and effort and sacrifice, but most of us do not want to get that serious about our faith—or our Savior.

Please do not misunderstand. Salvation and heaven are by God's grace and mercy, both unmerited, and not by our works. If we are in the kingdom of God, it is only by the blood of the Lamb. His death and resurrection justified us; His Spirit brought us to life. But we also know the nature of this world in which we are supposed to be living for Christ. If we are serious about our Christian witness, the day may be near when we may be persecuted—even killed—for our faith. We should be stirred, as John was stirred, as we witness this vast company of God's saints in heaven who have come through earth's great tribulation.

I am not saying we are not Christians. I am only trying to find out why we are so far from revival and refreshing and renewal. I am only trying to determine why we are so far from recognizing the urgency of God's will laid upon us by the Holy Spirit.

## We must not be afraid of the cost

If we belong to Jesus Christ, we should never compromise our spiritual decisions on the basis of "What is this going to cost me?" We ought only to ask, "What is my spiritual duty and my spiritual privilege before God?"

I thank God for John's vision of a company of believers so large that the number could not be calculated. The bodies of many of them had been burned at the stake. They had been tossed to the lions. They had undergone slow, agonizing torture. They could have collaborated with the enemy of their souls. They could have compromised for the sake of expediency and comfort. Instead, they faced the firing squads, the torture, the many cruel instruments of death, the terror of pain and suffering—for Jesus' sake! "Therefore are they before the throne of God" (7:15). "They have washed their robes, and made them white in the blood of the Lamb" (7:14).

There is no limit to what God could do in our world if we would dare to surrender before Him with a commitment like this:

> Oh God, I hereby give myself to You. I give my family. I give my business. I give all I possess. Take all of it, Lord—and take me! I give myself in such measure that if it is necessary that I lose everything for your sake, let me lose it. I will not ask what the price is. I will ask only that I may be all that I ought to be as a follower and disciple of Jesus Christ, my Lord. Amen.

If even 300 of God's people became that serious, our world would never hear the last of it! They would influence the news. Their message would go everywhere like birds on the wing. They would set off a great revival of New Testament faith and witness.

God wants to deliver us from the easygoing, smooth and silky, fat and comfortable Christianity so fashionable today. I hope we are willing to let the truth get hold of us, even at the cost of rejection or embarrassment.

The faith of the heavenly overcomers cost them everything and gained them everything. What of our faith?

# 9.

# The Supernatural Acts in Revelation: "Blow Your Trumpets!"

And when he had opened the seventh seal, there was silence in heaven about the space of half an hour.

And I saw the seven angels which stood before God; and to them were given seven trumpets. And another angel came and stood at the altar, having a golden censer; and there was given unto him much incense, that he should offer it with the prayers of all saints upon the golden altar which was before the throne. And the smoke of the incense, which came with the prayers of the saints, ascended up before God out of the angel's hand. And the angel took the censer, and filled it with fire of the altar, and cast it into the earth: and there were voices, and thunderings, and lightnings, and an earthquake.

And the seven angels which had the seven trumpets prepared themselves to sound.

The first angel sounded, and there followed hail and fire mingled with blood, and they were cast upon the earth: and the third part of trees was burnt up, and all green grass was burnt up.

And the second angel sounded, and as it were a great
mountain burning with fire was cast into the sea: and the
third part of the sea became blood;

And the third part of the creatures which were in the
sea, and had life, died; and the third part of the ships
were destroyed.

And the third angel sounded, and there fell a great
star from heaven, burning as it were a lamp, and it fell
upon the third part of the rivers, and upon the fountains
of waters;

And the name of the star is called Wormwood: and
the third part of the waters became wormwood; and
many men died of the waters, because they were made
bitter.

And the fourth angel sounded, and the third part of
the sun was smitten, and the third part of the moon, and
the third part of the stars; so as the third part of them
was darkened, and the day shone not for a third part of
it, and the night likewise.

And I beheld, and heard an angel flying through the
midst of heaven, saying with a loud voice, Woe, woe,
woe, to the inhabiters of the earth by reason of the other
voices of the trumpet of the three angels, which are yet
to sound!

                                          Revelation 8:1-13

The human race has always been quick to blame the
world's disasters and tragedies—floods, famines, plagues
—on "natural causes." But in the end of the age when the
final judgments of God begin to fall, how long will it be
until people confess that there is another real, though invisible, force in operation? Truly the wrath of God will leave
no hiding place for sinning men and women.

We are told by John the apostle of the mighty trumpets God gives to the seven angels "who stand before

[him]," and of the dreadful woes descending upon the earth as the trumpets begin to sound. I link these events to the climactic period throughout the earth when the antichrist has prevailed by means of deceit and force, enslaving the major portion of the world and violating every natural and spiritual law. Even then, as the judgments of God are being felt, I have no doubt that people will offer "rational explanations" for what is transpiring and logical excuses for their not taking heed.

God has spoken to us in a variety of ways. Our general response has been, "We did not hear His voice. We did not hear anything!" John recorded in his gospel the reactions of an audience who heard God speak audibly. When Jesus talked of His coming death, asking God to glorify His name through it, "then came there a voice from heaven, saying, I have both glorified it, and will glorify it again" (John 12:28). And what were the reactions of the bystanders? "The people therefore, that stood by, and heard it, said that it thundered: others said, An angel spake to him" (12:29).

People prefer their logic, their powers of reason. Even when God speaks, they refuse to recognize His voice. They will not confess that God has spoken through Jesus Christ, the eternal Son. When He confronts them with their sin, they consult a psychiatrist and hope they can get their personalities "properly adjusted." But in a coming day, every knee will bow and every tongue will confess that Jesus Christ is Lord of all.

First, however, the trumpets of God will have sounded!

## A supernatural transfer

This time, there will be no question in people's minds. When God shakes loose the world from Satan's control, shakes it loose from the rational scientists and the expedient politicians, shakes it loose from the pleasure lovers, He will turn it over to the One to whom it belongs—Jesus Christ! And He will do this in such a way that it will say to everyone on the earth: "This is a supernatural manifestation! This is the God of the entire universe speaking!"

When God is finally ready to refine and restore the earth, everyone in heaven and on earth and in hell will know that no human laboratory could compound the fire that will be poured out on the earth. God has promised that He will not hide His wrath forever. He is prepared to speak. And when He does, men will know that Oak Ridge scientists or Russian technologists could not produce these woes.

But before we come to God's judgments on our world, I need to make an important observation concerning the prayers of the people of God. Frequently I have heard Christians admit, "I am discouraged. I have prayed and prayed—and nothing has happened!"

John sees an angel with a golden censer standing at the heavenly altar. He was given "much incense," which he offered "with the prayers of all saints" on the golden altar before the heavenly throne (8:3). And "the smoke of the incense, which came with the prayers of the saints, ascended up before God out of the angel's hand."

It is right and proper that we who are the people of God should be giving ourselves to prayer. In Matthew 6:9-10, we read that Jesus taught His disciples to pray:

> Our Father which art in heaven,
> Hallowed be thy name.
> Thy kingdom come,
> Thy will be done in earth,
>     as it is in heaven.

Ever since, the believing saints of God have been praying the disciples' prayer: "Your kingdom come." That prayer cannot be answered—God's kingdom cannot come on earth—until God has shaken loose the usurpers who hold this world in their power and control. But in God's time the world will be restored to Jesus Christ who created it and bought it back with His own precious blood.

## A delayed response

I sense in this picture in Revelation that some of our prayers on that altar have been acknowledged, but God has purposely delayed His response. Those yet unanswered prayers of ours are being kept there at the altar that they may be mingled with the divine incense and thus become effective before God's throne. And now at last the moment has come. It is time for the fire from the altar to be hurled upon the earth as God's judgments continue.

There is still much about prayer and intercession that we do not understand. Probably we will continue to feel that our prayers often seem to be ineffective. It is my counsel, based on this episode, that our prayers are useful to God and effective. But God, for His own purposes, may hold them for all time before He answers.

Think of the kernels of grain, the seed, that the farmer plants in the ground in the fall of the year. How patient the farmer must be! Throughout the long, cold winter the seed is dormant. There is no evidence at all that it is there—covered by the cold earth itself. The snows come and go. The ground freezes and thaws. Does the farmer lie awake at night worrying that those seeds he placed in the ground may be ineffective? He does not. He knows that spring will come!

And in due course, the sunshine of March or April warms the air. Spring rains water the ground. The farmer knows then that it will not be long until green shoots suddenly break out from their covering of earth. And in their own time, great waving fields of grain are ready for the harvest. The farmer's faith in the seed he planted is fully justified.

Likewise, God wants us to be patient with every prayer and petition we sincerely send up to that heavenly altar. Our praying done in the Spirit cannot be ineffective. It is as though God is saying to us: "You have planted the seed. You have prayed for My will to be done and for My kingdom to come on earth. Your prayers will be mingled with the divine incense. The fire from the altar will fall upon the earth, and God's desire will be communicated to men and women. The effective prayers of my Son, Jesus, will join with the effective prayers of righteous men and women. Be patient and put your trust in Me, day by day!"

## The unexplained silence

You will note, as we return to the opening verse of chapter 8, that after the seventh seal was opened "there was silence in heaven for about half an hour." It will do you no good to ask me, "What does this silence in heaven mean?" I would tell you if I knew—but I do not know. It does indicate a pause, perhaps a kind of divine "Selah" in heaven, as though the wheels of judgment have ground to a merciful stop for a brief time.

John himself does not try to explain or interpret the heavenly silence. Instead, he proceeds to the next event in his vision: "And I saw the seven angels which stood before God; and to them were given seven trumpets ... And there were voices, and thunderings, and lightnings, and an earthquake" (8:2, 5).

John describes this heavenly phenomena taking place even before the seven angels sounded their trumpets of woe. Earlier, in his vision of the heavenly throne, John reported the "lightnings and thunderings and voices" that came from the throne (4:5). I believe John is telling us in chapter 8 that the heavenly manifestations of justice and judgment first seen and heard at the throne of God have now reached the earth. The crucial time of trial and tribulation for mankind has come.

It is well for us to review here what we know about the trumpets of God in the Bible. The blowing of trumpets is mentioned in the Scriptures 125 times. God instructed His people Israel to use trumpets for warnings, to call an assembly and to announce the feast days. Trumpets were also to be used to mobilize for war. The Old Testament prophets, speaking by the Spirit of God, used the figure of the sounding trumpet in their appeals to a backslidden nation: "Blow the trumpet in Zion: sound the alarm, warn the people!"

Paul, addressing the Corinthian believers concerning the end of the age and the return of Christ for His living saints and the resurrected Christian dead, had this to say:

> Behold, I shew you a mystery; We shall not all sleep, but we shall all be changed, In a moment, in the twinkling of an eye, at the last trump: for the trumpet shall sound, and the dead shall be raised incorruptible, and we shall be changed. (1 Corinthians 15:51-52)

## Why the talk of judgment?

Men and women, absorbed in their human contentment, will ask, "Why should there be the sounding trumpets? Why should there be such warnings? Why the talk of impending judgment?"

I will tell you why. God once walked and conversed with the man and woman He had created. He spoke to them in the Garden of Eden in the cool of the day in the quiet voice of love. And the man and the woman, walking among the trees of the garden, heard His voice and responded.

But Adam and Eve sinned, and since then their descendants have chosen not to listen for God's voice. Men and women could hear the voice of God if they would. By choice they do not.

As we noted earlier, lost humanity's cup of iniquity is brim full. The figure is alarming, frightening. God watches as the cup fills. Then, suddenly, it is an overflowing cup, and God summons His seven trumpeters to action:

> The first angel sounded, and there followed hail and fire mingled with blood, and they were cast upon the earth: and the third part of trees was burnt up, and all green grass was burnt up. (8:7)

People have always loved fire, and God will say, "Blow the trumpet—and give them all the fire they want!"

> And the second angel sounded, and as it were a great mountain burning with fire was cast into the sea: and the third part of the sea became blood; And the third part of the creatures which were in the sea, and had life, died; and the third part of the ships were destroyed. (8:8-9)

People have always been prone to shed the blood of their fellows, and God will say, "Blow the trumpet—and give them all the blood they can take!"

> And the third angel sounded, and there fell a great star from heaven, burning as it were a lamp, and it fell upon the third part of the rivers, and upon the fountains of waters; And the name of the star is called Wormwood: and the third part of the waters became wormwood; and many men died of the waters, because they were made bitter. (8:10-11)

People have always dealt with each other in bitterness. God will say, "Blow the trumpet—and give them bitterness, even more bitterness than they want!"

> And the fourth angel sounded, and the third part of the sun was smitten, and the third part of the moon, and the third part of the stars; so as the third part of them was darkened, and the day shone not for a third part of it, and the night likewise. (8:12)

People have always loved their deeds of darkness. God will say, "Blow the trumpet—and give them darkness and confusion and woe!"

## Judgments beyond mankind's doing

For sure, these will be manifestations of the wrath and the power of God that cannot be mistaken for anything humans are capable of doing. I wonder about some of the human presumptions in our day. I wonder—but I do not have the answers. I wonder if some of God's judgments will take place because of our arrogant presumptions inherent in our invasions into God's creation secrets, including the realm of space.

I do not have any scriptural grounds for saying this, but I do wonder if God will finally take His sponge, apply His own divine detergent and mop not only earth but sky, cleansing space of its human contamination.

As if the previous four judgments were insufficient, God issues a warning concerning what follows. John says,

> And I beheld, and heard an angel flying through the midst of heaven, saying with a loud voice, Woe, woe, woe, to the inhabiters of the earth by reason of the other voices of the trumpet of the three angels, which are yet to sound! (8:13)

All of what I have reviewed in this chapter pertains to an awesome day yet future. By the goodness and the grace of God, you and I today are not hearing those trumpet blasts of final woe and judgment.

Today we hear an entirely different voice. It is the voice of Jesus calling wandering sinners home, assuring them that God is still honoring repentance and faith and obedience! It is the voice of Jesus, as gentle as the voice of a mother calling to her firstborn. He says, "Come unto me, all ye that labour and are heavy laden" (Matthew 11:28).

## God intends for us to hear

Fellow Christian, it is God's will and God's plan that we hear His voice. It is the voice of Jesus, the voice of the Holy Spirit and the counsel of the Scriptures that we should not be overcome with the complexities and cares of our daily lives.

> Heaven and earth shall pass away: but my words shall not pass away.

> And take heed to yourselves, lest at any time your
> hearts be overcharged with surfeiting, and drunkenness,
> and cares of this life, and so that day come upon you
> unawares. For as a snare shall it come on all them that
> dwell on the face of the whole earth. (Luke 21:33-35)

Doctors warn us that we North Americans eat too much,
drink too much, sleep too much, worry too much. More
of us suffer from mental illness than suffer from major
physical illness. We are selfish and self-centered. We
want too many pleasures and too few responsibilities.
We who are believers are prone to think we will hear the
trumpets of woe in time to do something about all of
this. But at that time, it will be too late!

The voice of God today is a quiet voice. The voice of
God's love and grace is constant—never strident, never
compulsive. God has sent His messengers to every generation. He has spoken through the urgent voice of the
prophet. He has spoken through the concerned voice of
the preacher and the evangelist. He has spoken through
the sweet voice of the gospel singer. He has spoken
through the voices of plain, sincere, loving men and
women who have given faithful witness to the transforming new birth from above and the joys that God's
children will know throughout the eternity to come.

These voices from God have consistently proclaimed:

> Awake thou that sleepest,
> and arise from the dead,
> and Christ shall give thee light. (Ephesians 5:14)

These voices repeat the offer of our Lord: "Take my yoke
upon you, and learn of me; for I am meek and lowly in
heart: and ye shall find rest unto your souls" (Matthew
11:28).

## I am a troubled pastor

I confess that, as a pastor, I am a troubled man. I am concerned. It is too late in my ministry for me to be engaged week after week with men and women who do not hear the pleading voice of God for our time and for our condition. I am serious about this. I do wonder if God must turn from those who have heard all of the Bible truths over and over again in order to find willing and responsive listeners elsewhere.

In our basic evangelicalism we disagree with that. We assure ourselves that God is always waiting to bless us. I remind you that the Jews of Jesus' day held to the same attitude. "Do not worry about us," they said in effect. "We are Abraham's descendants. We know who we are. If God is going to bless anyone, He is going to bless us!" Remember what Jesus said to them: "If ye were Abraham's children, ye would do the works of Abraham" (John 8:39). If they were Abraham's descendants, He was saying, they would act like Abraham and not be trying to kill their promised Messiah.

I cannot determine when I will die. But I hope I do not live to see the day when God has to turn from men and women who have heard His holy truth and have played with it, fooled with it and equated it with fun and entertainment and religious nonsense.

We cannot deny that this attitude is found in much of current Christianity. As a result, people have hardened their hearts to the point that they no longer hear the voice of God.

We ought to be crying out in repentance and prayer: "O God, we have heard so much of Your truth, over and over again, yet we are ashamed that we have done so little in giving You our devotion and obedience!"

May God have mercy on us!

# 10.

# The Human Resolution in Revelation: "We Will Not Repent!"

And the fifth angel sounded, and I saw a star fall from heaven unto the earth: and to him was given the key of the bottomless pit. And he opened the bottomless pit; and there arose a smoke out of the pit, as the smoke of a great furnace; and the sun and the air were darkened by reason of the smoke of the pit. And there came out of the smoke locusts upon the earth: and unto them was given power, as the scorpions of the earth have power. And it was commanded them that they should not hurt the grass of the earth, neither any green thing, neither any tree; but only those men which have not the seal of God in their foreheads. And to them it was given that they should not kill them, but that they should be tormented five months: and their torment was as the torment of a scorpion, when he striketh a man. And in those days shall men seek death, and shall not find it; and shall desire to die, and death shall flee from them . . .

And the sixth angel sounded, and I heard a voice from the four horns of the golden altar which is before God, Saying to the sixth angel which had the trumpet, Loose the four angels which are bound in the great river Euphrates. And the four angels were loosed, which were prepared for an hour, and a day, and a month, and a year, for to slay the third part of men. And the number of the army of the horsemen were two hundred thousand thousand: and I heard the number of them . . .

And the rest of the men which were not killed by these plagues yet repented not of the works of their hands, that they should not worship devils, and idols of gold, and silver, and brass, and stone, and of wood: which neither can see, nor hear, nor walk.

Revelation 9:1-6, 13-16, 20

Everything I read these days tells me we are experiencing a great new wave of interest in spiritism and devil worship. I take this as one of the signs that God's age of grace and mercy is approaching the end point. It is evidence that the time may be near when He proclaims: "I have seen enough of mankind's sin, rebellion and perversion. It is time for the trumpets of judgment to sound!"

John's record in the ninth chapter of the Revelation is a somber, disturbing portrayal of judgment. It is a prophecy of destruction and desolation that cannot be anything but revolting to humans who deny that God has any right to judge and punish their rebellion against His love and His will. To us who believe that God is good and that He originally made us in His image, we discern a further message. He is saying that there is another world, another kingdom, that is always keeping an eye on this world we inhabit!

If we are willing to add this message from the Revelation to the weight of other Scriptures, we discover God saying to us that the earth on which we live is not self-explanatory and certainly not self-sufficient. This earth on which we spin is only a shadow of the real, though invisible, world above. Although our earth is largely peopled by a rebel race, it had a divine origin. And God is about to enforce His claim upon it and judge those who are usurpers.

Humans, deceived by the devil and charmed by their own pride and abilities, deny that our world is a rebel province in God's universe. They deny that human society has willfully pulled loose from God's rule and the rest of God's domain. In fact, they deny that men and women are the creation of God. They deny even that they owe any allegiance to God, their Creator.

Worst of all, in my opinion, these rebels deny that they will be obliged to settle their debt with the Creator God at a time of His choosing!

## The final settlement

John has been able to give us some indication of conditions and events that will take place on the earth as the hour of final settlement begins. He makes it clear that the visitation of judgment upon the earth will involve an invasion of supernatural powers. There will be fearsome creatures loosed upon the earth, and great segments of the population will not only suffer but will be slain in the process. Think together with me about the supernatural events.

I will have to confess that I am among those who have been consistently skeptical of the stories of "flying saucers." Likewise, I have never believed the tales people have told of sighting monstrous sea serpents. Although I have heard the legends concerning the diminutive leprechauns, I have never accepted the notion of their existence.

But I do believe that the supernatural is a part of God's being and eternal existence. I am convinced that when the living Lord of Creation, the Almighty God, begins to bring this rebel world back into the divine orbit, there will be an invasion from the world above as well as from the world below. And once the trumpets have sounded, sinful men and women will have no recourse. Neither will they have questions as to the origin of the judgment. There will be no need for a governmental inquiry or investigation. All will know that they have come to the time of God's judgment throughout the world.

As God sends these strange, punishing creatures upon the earth, there will be two human reactions. Some people will attempt suicide—only to discover that suicide is impossible: They "shall desire to die, and death shall flee from them" (9:6). Some will continue stubbornly in their sinful practices: "[They] yet repented not, that they should not worship devils, and idols, . . . neither repented they of their murders, nor of their sorceries, nor of their fornication, nor of their thefts" (9:20-21).

The God of heaven and earth, as He makes His just claims, will be saying to a rebellious, lost race: "You speak of the great 'natural' forces you have experienced. You know about the release of nuclear power and boast of your intelligence in discovering the secrets of fusion and fission. But as your Creator, I am forewarning you that you have not seen anything at all. Although you have become used to living in the midst of sin and violence in a tear-stained and terror-filled world, you have not seen anything to compare with the blood and fire and devastation and death that will signal the end of My grace and mercy!"

## Specific details omitted

John does not give us some of the specific details. For
example, we cannot here pinpoint the time of the rapture
of the believing church. John does give us one clue, however—the locust-like creatures with scorpion stingers
were instructed not to hurt men and women who had the
seal of God in their foreheads. The living saints will be
marked and protected for the little time they will yet be
on earth. But the wicked and the unbelieving will be tormented by these invading creatures until they will want
to die. And even that desperate respite will be denied
them—they will not even be able to "end it all."

In John's vision, there was a sixth trumpet blast. John
heard a voice coming from the horns of the golden altar
before God, saying, "Loose the four angels" (9:14). And
the four angels who had been in readiness for this
moment were released "to slay the third part of man."
They accomplished their gruesome assignment by
means of an "army of the horsemen" numbering "two
hundred thousand thousand." John adds: "The heads of
the horses were as the heads of lions; and out of their
mouths issued fire and smoke and brimstone. By these
three was the third part of men killed, by the fire, and by
the smoke, and by the brimstone, which issued out of
their mouths."

Now, I am aware that there are many people—even
some Christians—who do not believe these judgments
and torments will actually happen. They may discount
the Revelation, arguing that the imagery is hard to interpret, but what will they do with the words and warnings
of our Lord Jesus Christ? Here is what He said:

> Take heed that no man deceive you . . . And ye shall
> hear of wars and rumours of wars: see that ye be not

troubled . . . nation shall rise against nation, and kingdom against kingdom: and there shall be famines, and pestilences, and earthquakes, in divers places. All these are the beginning of sorrows . . .

Then shall they deliver you up to be afflicted, and shall kill you: and ye shall be hated of all nations for my name's sake. And then shall many be offended, and shall betray one another, and shall hate one another . . .

For then shall be great tribulation, such as was not since the beginning of the world to this time, no, nor ever shall be. And except those days should be shortened, there should no flesh be saved: but for the elect's sake those days shall be shortened . . .

Immediately after the tribulation of those days shall
the sun be darkened,
and the moon shall not give her light,
and the stars shall fall from heaven,
and the powers of the heavens shall be shaken."

(Matthew 24:4-29)

## Confirmed by prophets and apostles

Students of the Bible are aware that the Old Testament prophets and the writing apostles of New Testament times foresaw and proclaimed God's coming day of judgment—the consummate settling of accounts between the sovereign God and His rebellious and sinful creation.

Throughout the centuries, saints whom God has touched with the heavenly fire from His altar have woven this concept of accountability and judgment into a discernible tapestry. In our day, we have seen the vision dimly, and we can only confess that we do not understand

it all. I have said it before. Let us not get involved in trying
to decipher all the minute details of God's plans. The great
central truth is what matters: When God gets enough of
this world's sin and violence and rebellion, He will do
something about it!

God intends to restore the unity of His creation. He
will sort out good from bad. He will halt the infection of
evil. He will balance the scales of justice.

Jesus Christ revealed to John the broad outline of
God's wrathful judgment. We sense a progression in
the breaking of the seals, in the sounding of the trumpets, in the pouring out of the vials, in the appearance
of the four horsemen. We do not need to know the
details. God has said He will use every means to shake
loose the rebellious forces that have laid claim to His
earth.

How desperately we would like to believe that in the
face of such worldwide judgments, all lost men and
women will cry out to God, "We have been wrong! We
repent! We confess our evil deeds! We want to join those
whose faith and trust is in God!"

I repeat: We would like to believe that judgment will
bring unbelievers to God. But such will not be the case.
"The rest of the men which were not killed by these
plagues yet repented not" (9:20).

## Repentance is our moral obligation

All my adult life I have been a student of the Bible.
Among other things, it is the record of how God deals
with mankind. I can draw but one conclusion from my
research: All people are morally obligated to repent
and to ask forgiveness of God. Failing to do that, they
will perish. In the course of my ministry I have talked

to people who thought they would be doing God a big favor if they would repent. The fact is, men and women who repent and return to God are simply doing what they should do as beings once created in God's likeness.

It should not be a surprise to us when John reports that people who have just seen a third of the world's population perish in divine judgment will continue to rebel against God. We live amid a proud, selfish and self-sufficient people. Even in our Christian churches there are those who want to be known as "respectable church members"—and not as lost sinners who have had to confess their guilt before God. How infrequently do we hear of genuine repentance! When repentance is real and faith is genuine, the atoning death of Jesus Christ is effective for pardon.

But the sad lesson from the Scriptures is plain. Sinful, rebellious people can never be forced to repent. The same act that may cause one person to repent and believe will cause others to hate and despise God. The same Bible sermon that brings one person to tearful submission at an altar of prayer will send others out with pride and a resolve to have their own human way.

If we are close enough to God in our spiritual life and desires, we want Him to do something about present-day lawless rebellion. We recognize it as blasphemy against the high King of Heaven. But even some Christians do not want God to do anything that will bring judgment or suffering. Can we be unconcerned about bringing this world to a final accounting before God? If our hearts beat with the heart of God, should we not cry out within ourselves, "O God, do send Your judgments! Let Your judgments be revealed in Your time and in Your own measure!"

## There are things worse than death

Death is not the worst thing that can happen to a person. I recall the first time I heard that statement. I was in a quiet conversation with Harry M. Shuman, for many years president of The Christian and Missionary Alliance. He was a soft-spoken, yet forceful man of God, rich in the wisdom of God's Word. We were talking of the serious issues of life and death. When he had something especially important to say, Dr. Shuman had an unusual way of lowering his voice and tilting his head just a bit. I can see him yet as he looked out from under his shaggy brows straight into my eyes. "Remember, Tozer, death is not the worst thing that can happen to a person!"

For the Christian, death is a journey to the eternal world. It is a victory, a rest, a delight. I am sure my small amount of physical suffering in life has been mild compared with Paul's. But I think I have some understanding of what he meant when he told the Philippians: "For to me to live is Christ, and to die is gain . . . [I] desire to depart, and to be with Christ; which is far better" (Philippians 1:21, 23). The more a Christian suffers in the body, the more he or she thinks about the triumph of going home to heaven.

But we modern Christians seem to be a strange breed. We are so completely satisfied with the earthly things we have collected, and we so enjoy this age's creature comforts, that we would rather stay here for a long, long time! Probably we do not tell God about that kind of desire when we pray. We know it would not be considered pious or spiritual if people knew we preferred our position here to the prospect of heaven.

For years I have made a practice of writing many of my earnest prayers to God in a little book—a book now well worn. I still turn often to the petitions I recorded in that book. I remind God often of what my prayers have been.

One prayer in the book—and God knows it well by this time, for I pray it often—goes like this:

> Oh God,
> Let me die rather than to go on day by day living wrong. I do not want to become a careless, fleshly old man. I want to be right so that I can die right. Lord, I do not want my life to be extended if it would mean that I should cease to live right and fail in my mission to glorify You all of my days!

## An Old Testament example

Long ago, Hezekiah, king of Judah, became ill and God told him he would die. The king turned his face to the wall and sulked. Then he asked the Lord, in effect, "Why me? I have cleansed the temple, and we have had a revival. Because of me, the nation has come closer to You."

As you will recall from 2 Kings 20, the Lord gave Hezekiah a 15-year extension of life. Restored to health and vigor, Hezekiah disgraced himself and dishonored God before he died and was buried.

I would not want an extra 15 years in which to backslide and dishonor my Lord. I would rather go home right now than to live on—if living on was to be a waste of God's time and my own!

We look at the deteriorating condition of our world. We consider the godless lifestyles of so many millions of the world's people. Then we reflect on the devastating future judgments prophesied in the Revelation and elsewhere in God's Word. Harry M. Shuman was right: For the sincere followers of the Lamb, death is not the worst thing that can happen to them.

# 11.

# The Command in Revelation: "No More Delay!"

And I saw another mighty angel come down from heaven, clothed with a cloud: and a rainbow was upon his head, and his face was as it were the sun, and his feet as pillars of fire: And he had in his hand a little book open: and he set his right foot upon the sea, and his left foot on the earth, And cried with a loud voice, as when a lion roareth: and when he had cried, seven thunders uttered their voices. And when the seven thunders had uttered their voices, I was about to write: and I heard a voice from heaven saying unto me, Seal up those things which the seven thunders uttered, and write them not.

And the angel which I saw stand upon the sea and upon the earth lifted up his hand to heaven, And sware by him that liveth for ever and ever, who created heaven, and the things that therein are, and the earth, and the things that therein are, and the sea, and the things which are therein, that there should be time no longer: But in the days of the voice of the seventh angel, when he shall begin to sound, the mystery of God should be finished, as he hath declared to his servants the prophets.

Revelation 10:1-7

If you have ever watched a basketball or a football game, you know that when a team calls "Time out!" there will be a pause, a time of waiting. If the coach or manager wants to communicate a message to the players, he calls "Time out!" At that point, everything comes to a temporary halt. That is the rule of the contest.

The game clock stops. The ball is inactive. There can be no scoring. "Time out!" is a period of waiting until the referee blows the whistle, calling the players back to their positions so that the game can continue. When that whistle blows, the referee actually is announcing, "There will be no more delay!"

I use that illustration to make plain the meaning of the activity related in Revelation 10. One of God's mighty angels proclaims to the entire creation: "There will be no more delay! The God who lives for ever and ever, the God who created the heavens and the earth and the sea, will now bring to pass all that He has planned on behalf of His creation. There will be no more delay!"

For years we have read this announcement in the King James Version of the Bible, where the wording is "There should be time no longer." In our hymns and gospel songs we have made wide use of that phrase, singing about time being no more, looking forward to a period when time will cease. But actually, that great angel messenger was proclaiming, "The time-out is ending. The long pause is over. There will be no more delay. The living God is now prepared to reveal the consummation of all things!"

Now, if any of us who believe the Bible and are expecting the Lord's return should be granted an audience before the United Nations assembly and should start to explain God's plan for the consummation of this age, we would be booed and hooted out of that impressive hall! We would quickly be evicted—and not just by atheistic Russians or Chinese, but by American, Canadian and British delegates, too! We will never get a hearing at the United Nations for God's plans. But the prophetic word of David and Isaiah and Daniel and Paul and Peter still stands. These men were not mistaken in their faith. And, thankfully, the words of our Lord Jesus Christ will stand!

## Daniel predicted the consummation

Consider God's last words to Daniel at the end of his prophetic record. By then, Daniel was old and weary, but all his life he had been God's faithful servant. God said:

> And he said, Go thy way, Daniel: for the words are closed up and sealed till the time of the end. Many shall be purified, and made white, and tried; but the wicked shall do wickedly: and none of the wicked shall understand; but the wise shall understand. And from the time that the daily sacrifice shall be taken away, and the abomination that maketh desolate set up, there shall be a thousand two hundred and ninety days. Blessed is he that waiteth, and cometh to the thousand three hundred and five and thirty days. But go thou thy way till the end be: for thou shalt rest, and stand in thy lot at the end of the days. (Daniel 12:9-13)

As far as we know, Daniel died a natural death. But many of the prophets died violent deaths because of their faith. Consider, too, the Christian martyrs of the past centuries. You should be familiar with their lives, if you are not. Their testimonies will always stand. They forfeited physical life in the calm and joyful belief that

God is faithful and that He will make all things right in
the consummation that is yet ahead. They knew that sin
and greed and hatred were in control for a time, but their
destination was their Father's house, and they knew that
everything up there has always been all right!

These martyrs were aware that God had called a
"Time out!" for His own good reasons. It was not that
God had abandoned His plan, worked out from the
foundation of the world. His plan is perfect—God's
nature assures us of that, even as we wait. This present
delay is a time of mercy, a window of salvation.

God's great plan for the salvation of our lost race
deals with mankind's sinfulness and with God's own
holiness and justice. There can be little argument about
what sin has done to the human race. The Bible speaks
of our life as a cup with a certain capacity. As long as we
sin against God, the cup continues to fill. We sin and we
sin and we sin! We seem to be of the opinion that God
does not really take notice of our rebellion against Him.

But the sins are cumulative. That is the terrible thing
about transgression. Sin in the human nature builds. It
grows and grows. Finally our propensity for evil reaches
the point of overflow, and then the judgment of God
must fall.

There was a time in history when the wickedness of
the nations had built to the point of overflow. God's
righteous judgment should have fallen on all of mankind. But at that crucial point in time, Jesus Christ, the
eternal Son, the Lamb of God Himself came to earth and
gave His life, opening wide the gates of heaven.
Through the atoning death of our Savior, God was able
to extend pardon to all who came to Jesus in faith,
appealing for mercy.

The God of all mercy in effect called a divine "Time
out!" While His eternal Son is actively interceding at His

right hand, God's cataclysmic judgment upon our world will be delayed.

Bible scholars call the 10th chapter of the Revelation "parenthetical." By that they mean that, although significant, it does not advance the progress of events in the entire book. But as I ponder this heavenly scene, my heart is lifted up! I do not know what it does for you, but it gets me out of the dull earth, where cares abound, and transports me into another world. I do not have to understand it all to be blessed and helped. The Revelation is rich, rewarding, awesome! It is at once magnificent and terrible, noble and frightening.

We must not lose sight of the fact that this record primarily is the revelation of Jesus Christ. When you look up into the heavens at night, you may see an especially bright star, but you cannot help seeing as well many of the other stars surrounding it. In the Revelation we have primarily the revelation of Jesus Christ Himself. He is first. He is "of the Father's love begotten." Jesus is the One by whom the race is to be redeemed, the earth restored, evil vanquished, Satan defeated, justice established, the alienation between God and us ended. Jesus split apart the curtain that separated us from God.

Yet, when we look fully at Jesus, we see also much that surrounds Him. We take note, for instance, of the angels of heaven, the reality of hell and the great abyss, the throne of God, the souls of the righteous, the last judgment, the marriage supper of the Lamb, the new heavens and the new earth.

## Do not be frightened by the symbols

I have mentioned before the use of symbols in the Revelation. Figures of speech abound throughout the

Bible. We should not let the use of symbolism frighten us away. That is one of the devil's neatest tricks—getting believers to suppose there is so much in the Word of God that they cannot understand that they neglect all of the Word of God. My advice: Go to the Bible itself. You will find that it interprets itself.

For example, John saw the angel "robed in a cloud." Do you suppose that could be a cloud as we know clouds? Clouds are composed of water. They make poor robes. But go back into the life and history of Israel, God's chosen people. In the wilderness Israel followed the divine cloud by day and the pillar of fire by night. The cloud and the fire were the "Shekinah"—the presence of Almighty God with His pilgrim people. That was the glory of God. Again, when the risen Christ was taken away into heaven, a cloud received Him out of their sight. In the Scriptures a cloud means the visible manifestation of the invisible God.

When this mighty angel came forth from the throne of God, John saw his robe as that of a cloud. Something of the splendor and glory of God at His throne clung to the angel as he moved from the heavenly scene to command the judgments of God on the earth. There was a rainbow above his head. His face was like the sun. His legs were like fiery pillars. As a mighty messenger from God, he planted his right foot on the sea and his left foot on the land. When he shouted, it was like the roar of a lion, and in the midst of it all, John heard as well the voices of "the seven thunders" (10:3).

John tells us he was about to write down what the seven thunders said, but a voice from heaven ordered, "Seal up those things which the seven thunders uttered" (10:4). Some people are curious as to the message of the seven thunders. They have a hard time letting the matter rest. They want to know.

I have a feeling that sometime in our eternal future we are going to know the message spoken by the thunders. For now, we must leave it at that. It was a message sealed up for a later time. Of one thing I am confident: it was a message spoken in favor of God and His Christ; it was a message on the side of righteousness, faithfulness and holiness.

Do you not think God expects us to focus on the more important issues? Why should we spend time over obscure, curious elements? God has given us 66 books within our Bible to prepare us for the coming events that will signal the return of Christ and the judgment of the nations. Heeding what we know to do will keep us well occupied.

## Decisive action

The mighty angel whom John saw raised his right hand to the heavens. He knew the time had come. He knew authority had been given to him. He raised his right hand in acknowledgment of the God above whom he worshiped and served.

I like that! We have too many weak personalities on earth who always leave something undone. They are afraid to take final, decisive action. As a result, they do not accomplish the goals they have set. With the poet we say, "We are such little men when the stars come out!"

Yes, I like this picture John has given us. The mighty angel knows his task and his authority. He raises his right hand to heaven and in the name of the eternal God cries out, "The time has come! There will be no more delay!"

When the time comes for that announcement, three worlds will hear it. Heaven will hear it, with full agreement that the time of judgment has indeed come. The underworld of hell will hear the shout, and there will be fright. And on earth, the saints of God, the believing body of Christ, will hear it and be glad!

We are living in a period when God waits in grace and mercy. In His faithfulness, God is calling out a people for His name—those who will repent and believe, those who will cast their lot with Jesus Christ. When the mighty angel shouts his signal and raises his hand heavenward, it will be eternally too late. Only God can say when iniquity overflows, when the time is ripe.

The event is certain; its timing is uncertain. Those facts constitute one of the compelling reasons for my strong belief in the cause of world missions. I am thankful to be a part of a missionary-minded church. I believe involvement in God's program of calling out a people worldwide for His name is of primary importance. The church is not simply a religious institution. It is not religious theater where performers are paid to amuse those who attend. It is an assembly of redeemed sinners—men and women called unto Christ and commissioned to spread His gospel to the ends of the earth.

Then, at a time known only to God, the end of the age will come and Jesus Christ will return to earth for His own believing and faithful people—His church.

## Yes, Jesus Christ will return

I am not surprised that I still meet people who do not believe in the return of Christ. Some of them, in fact, armed with Bibles, would like to set me straight. Not too long after an editorial appeared in which I quoted the apostle Paul, I heard from a professor who told me I had it all wrong. Paul did not mean what I had said he meant as I applied his statement to present day life.

I took time to write a reply. "When it comes to saying what he meant," I began, "Paul's batting average has been pretty good up to now. So I will string along with what Paul plainly, clearly said." I did not figure I needed someone to straighten me out—especially someone who had decided the Bible does not mean what it says.

When the Bible says God is calling a special people out of the nations to bear His name, I believe it! When the Bible declares His name is Jesus and His people are Christians—Christ's ones—I believe that, too! No one is going to argue me out of my faith in what God has said. As far as I am concerned, it is a fact that Jesus is coming again. The question I raise is this: "Are we prepared spiritually for His coming? Are we tolerating conditions in our midst that will cause us embarrassment when He comes?

In the evangelical church, we have come through a period when nearly everyone believed and taught the same thing concerning our preparation for Christ's return. There has been just one prerequisite to readiness: being born again. Being born again is almost like receiving a pass to a special event. When Jesus returns, we whip out the pass to prove our readiness!

Frankly, I do not think it will be at all like that. I do not believe that all of the professed believers are automatically ready to meet the Lord. If being born again was the only prerequisite, I must ask why Peter and Paul and John and our Lord exhorted, warned, pleaded that we should live and watch and pray so as to be ready for Jesus' coming? If we are automatically ready, why does our Lord admonish the Philadelphia church to hold tenaciously to their faith and strength so "that no man take [their] crown" (3:11)?

## God demands spiritual preparation

Our pious forefathers believed in spiritual preparation, and they said so. They saw themselves as a bride being prepared to meet the bridegroom. They regarded this earth as the dressing room to outfit them for heaven. They were well aware of God's admonition to personal holiness even as He was holy.

I shall be frank. I do not believe God is going to allow His carnal, selfish children; His lustful, worldly minded children; His money-loving, pleasure-seeking children to come rushing pell-mell into His holy presence singing their gospel ditties. I do not!

Why are we so slow to admit that our Lord Jesus Christ taught that He would accomplish His great task of church building through spiritually gifted men and women? His New Testament promises are so plain that no one can misunderstand them. It was His word that we should "receive power" through the infusion of His Spirit in our lives.

When the "Time out!" ends, none of us should go limping and excuse-laden into the presence of the Lord. Can you imagine people standing before the sovereign God trying to explain why they messed up their Christian lives because they refused to let the Holy Spirit bestow the sweet graces and pleasant fruits of holiness that the Bible promises?

I have mentioned the necessity for spiritual preparation in light of the coming of our Lord Jesus Christ. Such preparation is related as well to spiritual responsibility. Too many professing Christians will not accept responsibility. They are woefully mistaken in their theology when they excuse themselves by insisting that "Jesus did all the dying and we get all the benefits—without any responsibility." I think they must have fallen short in their Bible study.

One aspect of Christ's coming is our solemn appearance before His judgment seat, at which time we shall "receive the things done in [our] body, according to that [we] hath done, whether it be good or bad"(2 Corinthians 5:10). What we have done for our own glory will be exposed to our embarrassment. Our supposed accomplishments achieved without the direction of the Holy Spirit will be blown away as worthless stubble. In that final day of review and examination, only that which has been wrought by the Spirit of God will endure as eternal treasure.

## The pursuit of godliness

It pains me every time I hear Christians excusing their shallow, carnal living with a "We're doing the best we can!" The apostle Peter told the suffering Christians of his day that there was a far better testimony than that:

> Seeing then that all these things shall be dissolved, what manner of persons ought ye to be in all holy conversation and godliness, looking for and hasting unto the coming of the day of God, wherein the heavens being on fire shall be dissolved, and the elements shall melt with fervent heat? . . .
>
> Be diligent that ye may be found of him in peace, without spot, and blameless . . .
>
> Beware lest ye also, being led away with the error of the wicked, fall from your own stedfastness. But grow in grace, and in the knowledge of our Lord and Saviour Jesus Christ. To him be glory both now and for ever. (2 Peter 3:11-18)

Perhaps in light of that exhortation you feel as I do: that we need to drop off even some of the "normal" things we are doing—things that may not of themselves be wrong, but things that are keeping us from the serious pursuit of godliness.

At that coming day, we shall not be sorry we did!

# 12.

# The Invitation in Revelation: "Eat and Digest God's Word!"

And the voice which I heard from heaven spake unto me again, and said, Go and take the little book which is open in the hand of the angel which standeth upon the sea and upon the earth. And I went unto the angel, and said unto him, Give me the little book. And he said unto me, Take it, and eat it up; and it shall make thy belly bitter, but it shall be in thy mouth sweet as honey.

And I took the little book out of the angel's hand, and ate it up; and it was in my mouth sweet as honey: and as soon as I had eaten it, my belly was bitter. And he said unto me, Thou must prophesy again before many peoples, and nations, and tongues, and kings.

Revelation 10:8-11

We are living in a time of soft, easy Christianity. It is an era marked by a polite, weekly "nibbling" around the edges of the Word of God. Our pews are filled with nice, affable Christians who are willing to listen to outlines from the Bible purporting to be sermons. But they fail to absorb and digest the Word so that it becomes their controlling interest.

Any study of the Revelation will fall short of God's purpose if it does not make us more keenly aware of the eternal, unchanging nature of God's Word to mankind. In God's realm, the saddest words of tongue or pen may well be, "I failed to take God at His word."

The 10th chapter of the Revelation concludes with the apostle John's testimony concerning a divine scroll. The divine scroll had to do with impending judgment upon our earth. The open scroll was in the hand of the strong angel who stood on land and sea. Instructed by a heavenly voice to ask for the open scroll, John did so. The angel was not only quite willing for John to have it, but he told John to eat the document, adding, "It will turn your stomach sour, but in your mouth it will be as sweet as honey." John followed the unusual instructions and found the angel's prediction accurate.

Now, a little scroll in John's day would be a little book in ours. So I am going to refer to the scroll as a book—a book of divine origin.

We have no way of knowing the full significance of the little book that John took from the hand of the angel. But there is considerable agreement among Bible students that it symbolizes the Word of God—or perhaps some particular part of the Word of God. Such an interpretation agrees with other prophetic Scripture.

## Jeremiah, Ezekiel

Jeremiah, for example, was given the difficult task of bearing word of God's impending judgment to Judah and Jerusalem. It would be an unwelcome message to those for whom it was destined:

For who shall have pity upon thee, O Jerusalem?
or who shall bemoan thee?
or who shall go aside to ask how thou doest?
Thou hast forsaken me, saith the LORD,
thou art gone backward:
therefore will I stretch out my hand against thee, and
     destroy thee;
I am weary with repenting. (Jeremiah 15:5-6)

Jeremiah was a willing messenger, but he was under no illusion concerning the response God's message would meet—or of his own vulnerability as the bearer of such tidings:

O LORD, thou knowest:
remember me, and visit me, and
revenge me of my persecutors;
take me not away in thy longsuffering:
know that for thy sake I have suffered rebuke. (15:15)

Then Jeremiah added this interesting statement:

Thy words were found, and I did eat them;
and thy word was unto me the joy and rejoicing of mine
     heart:
for I am called by thy name, O LORD God of hosts. (15:16)

Ezekiel had a similar experience when God commissioned him to prophesy to rebellious Israel:

And he said unto me, Son of man, stand upon thy feet, and I will speak unto thee. And the spirit entered into me when he spake unto me, and set me upon my feet, that I heard him that spake unto me. And he said unto me, Son of man, I send thee to the children of Israel, to a rebellious

> nation that hath rebelled against me: they and their
> fathers have transgressed against me, even unto this very
> day . . .
>
> And when I looked, behold, an hand was sent unto
> me; and, lo, a roll of a book was therein; And he spread
> it before me; and it was written within and without: and
> there was written therein lamentations, and mourning,
> and woe.
>
> Moreover he said unto me, Son of man, eat that thou
> findest; eat this roll, and go speak unto the house of
> Israel. So I opened my mouth, and he caused me to eat
> that roll. And he said unto me, Son of man, cause thy
> belly to eat, and fill thy bowels with this roll that I give
> thee. Then did I eat it; and it was in my mouth as honey
> for sweetness. And he said unto me, Son of man, go, get
> thee unto the house of Israel, and speak with my words
> unto them. (Ezekiel 2:1-3:4)

The word God asked Jeremiah and Ezekiel to deliver
was a bitter warning of divine judgment. But Jeremiah
testified that as he "ate" God's words they were "the joy
and rejoicing of mine heart." And Ezekiel, with similar
reaction concerning the scroll he had ingested, said, "It
was in my mouth as honey for sweetness."

## Similar terminology

Returning to John's account in Revelation 10, we find
similar circumstances and terminology. God has a
prophetic word for John to convey. It is a bitter word of
impending divine judgment. As he ingests the word, it is
honey sweet, but it turns his stomach sour.

Perhaps we have lost something in getting away
from the old King James's "bitter belly"—"As soon as I

had eaten it, my belly was bitter." There are "happy-happy-happy" people in our churches who will insist that the Word of God can never be anything but honey sweet. It is my contention, however, that the Christian believers who are intent upon being faithful witnesses for Jesus Christ are not destined to always find sweetness and light in their contacts with evil, rebellious people.

When we digest, absorb, soak up the Word of the Lord, it becomes part and parcel of our daily lives. It is our delight. It is honey and sweetness. But as we share that same Word in our witness to lost men and women, we will know something of the bitterness and hostility—even enmity—that was the experience of John and Jeremiah and Ezekiel. There have been times when I have had to counsel believers who had become discouraged to the point of despair because of the treatment they had received at the hands of those who hated their witness.

There is another sense in which the Word becomes bitterness within us. It becomes bitterness to our sinful nature, because the sinful nature "lusteth against the Spirit" (Galatians 5:17). There are people within our Christian fellowships who have determined to set their own agendas—to live their lives as they please. They expect to be recognized as Christians, but they will not bow to the controls God has built into His holy Word and will. They read their Bibles—they even buy a new Bible every few years. They have enough spiritual knowledge to know that the commitment of their spirit, soul and body to the standards of God's Word will mean some bitter housecleaning within. But they have decided to take no step that will bring pain or sharpness or harshness into what is now for them a soft and easy profession of the Christian life.

These people are determined to manage the influence of the Word of God in their lives rather than to allow the Word of God to manage them day by day, hour by hour.

## Not judgmental, but concerned

Some people have accused me of sitting in judgment. But I think I am examining, with Christian concern, the true spiritual condition of many within the church's ranks. There exists a mind-set within present-day Christianity that supposes no one should get into trouble or suffer embarrassment for Christ's sake.

What is our answer when the Holy Spirit whispers to us about the true nature of our professed love for Jesus Christ? Suppose a young man proclaims his love for a certain young woman and wants to have her for his wife. But there is a difficulty he must consider. The girl's father is hostile to the match, letting the young man know that if he shows up again, he may be invited to leave under threat of a baseball bat—or worse.

If that young man schemes of ways to see the girl regardless of her father's threats, I would call it a case of true love. But if he professes his love and then is frightened off by the threats, probably the girl was nothing more than a passing fancy.

I realize that my illustration has to do with human nature. Human nature is prone to measure the importance of benefits and to determine whether or not the benefits are worth the effort. Within our Christian setting, we presume we are talking about men and women who have been born again, brought out of darkness into light, transformed by the grace and mercy of God. They have tasted the benefits God has for them in Christ Jesus.

Throughout church history, millions of people have proven what it actually means to be loyal to Christ, what it means to say that Jesus Himself is more important than anything in this world.

## "They tore at me!"

A number of years ago, in Chicago, I was in a car with several young people on our way to a youth rally. One of those in the car was a Jewish girl. Why she was with that Christian group I do not know, except that God's Spirit was still doing something in her life and soul. She told us of her experience in giving her heart to Jesus Christ and receiving Him as her Messiah. But afterward, at home with her family and relatives, she encountered not only the traditional hatred for Jesus but actual physical abuse as well. I remember the chills I felt as she emotionally described how she was attacked.

"They tore at me! They screamed at me! They literally ripped my dress and clothes from my body and demanded that I repudiate my faith!"

"What did you do?" her young friends in the car asked.

I remember yet the anger in her answer. "What could I do? It wasn't worth it! It wasn't worth what I had to put up with!" Yet, there she was, going with Christian friends to a youth rally. I never heard more about the girl. Deep in my heart, I believe that if she truly had found Jesus as her Messiah and Lord, God had something further for her. I do not think her angry outburst of "It wasn't worth it" could have been the end of her faith.

I cannot describe what I feel deep within me when I hear of a Christian brother or sister who has suffered for the faith, or who has been martyred for the testimony of

Jesus Christ. As I said earlier, my church is deeply
involved in overseas missions. Just within the areas of
my church's responsibility, it would be impossible to say
how many faithful pastors and lay people have actually
died for the faith. With a sense of distant admiration, we
call them simple-hearted nationals. God calls them overcomers! Professing Christians in our North American
churches can hardly comprehend so costly a price for the
faith we take for granted. Material prosperity and popular acceptance have sapped the vitality of our witness.

It is a completely distorted view of true biblical faith
to personify Christianity by the wealthy, back-slapping
boisterous businessperson who measures success by
bank accounts, big cars, palatial homes and expensive
vacations. I certainly am not saying that successful and
prosperous people cannot be Christians—the grace and
mercy of God sees to that. My point is that Christianity,
in so many instances, is being equated with material
wealth and affluence. These are the conditions that are
facing us in Christianity, not only in North America but
in other nations as well.

## Have we "eaten the book"?

The question is this: What are we allowing the Word of
God to say to us, and what is our reaction to that Word?
Have we consumed and digested the book? Have we
absorbed the Word of God into our lives? Or are we
among those content to be a part of a Christian congregation where there are no extreme demands, where fellowship will be consistently pleasant and without
responsibility?

When we, as Christians, love our Lord Jesus Christ
with heart and soul and mind, the Word of God is on our

side! If we could only grasp the fact that God's Word is more than a book! It is the revelation of divine truth from the person of God Himself. It has come as a divine communication in the sacred Scriptures. It has come to us in the guidance and conviction imparted by the divine Spirit of God within our beings. It has been modeled for us in Jesus Christ, the incarnate Word and the eternal Son.

Probably the majority of people who have lived in this 20th century have held and hold to the idea that God is silent. I have talked with people who supposed that God spoke the holy Scriptures into being and then lapsed into centuries-long silence.

God is not silent, and His love for His creation is such that He has never been silent. We should realize, for the good of our spiritual lives, that the Scriptures are effective in our beings because the Living Word is speaking in heaven and the Living Voice is sounding throughout the earth:

> For this is the love of God, that we keep his commandments: and his commandments are not grievous. For whatsoever is born of God overcometh the world . . .
> And it is the Spirit that beareth witness, because the Spirit is truth. For there are three that bear record in heaven, the Father, the Word, and the Holy Ghost: and these three are one. And there are three that bear witness in earth, the Spirit, and the water, and the blood: and these three agree in one. If we receive the witness of men, the witness of God is greater: for this is the witness of God which he hath testified of his Son. He that believeth on the Son of God hath the witness in himself (1 John 5:3-10)

We who preach the Word of God do not have the facility for plain speech that the Holy Spirit imparted to

John. Can words be more direct than these? "This is love for God: to obey his commands."

The act of committal to Jesus Christ in salvation releases us from the penalty of sin, but it does not release any of us from the obligation to obey the words of Christ, our Savior. Rather, it brings us under the joyful necessity to obey. If we would have God's blessing upon us, we must begin to obey.

## Mankind has not heeded God's Word

In the Revelation we have noted again and again that God has been faithful in warning men and women that the end of this age will come and that the judgments of God will fall. In the vision given to John, it appears that the people of the last days had taken their own safety for granted. They were not disturbed about their future. Seemingly they ignored every indication that the God who created them was a person of His Word. As a result, they were totally unprepared for death, judgment and eternity.

Conditions in our churches cause me to believe that many professing Christians are living under a similarly false sense of security. The Old Testament prophets consistently warned Israel about false security. Israel supposed that because the nation was especially chosen by God, everything else would fall into place. Messiah would come. They would hail Him. He would set up His rule on earth. All that they took for granted. But Messiah came, and they did not recognize Him. Their own religious leaders conspired to have Him crucified. How many in Israel had recognized Him? One in a thousand? One in ten thousand?

There are two kinds of tranquility among us—not counting the tranquilizers a person can buy in bottles.

There is the tranquility that people find in just taking themselves and everything around them for granted. They tend to believe all kinds of good things about themselves—which are not really true. That is dangerous.

Then there is the true tranquility that God has promised when the soul has been shaken to its foundation. There is little preaching about this kind of tranquility in our day. Too often men and women get referred to psychiatrists rather than to God. If they would do what the Bible directs, they would take their disturbances and their alarms to God and to an open Bible. If the Holy Spirit is allowed to illuminate the Word of God, the Word will first do its surgery, but then it will mend what it has cut. The result is true tranquility of soul, spirit and mind.

## They say it does not make sense

To the worldling this does not make sense. "I will stick with the psychiatrist," is his or her response. But the necessity for spiritual illumination before we can grasp spiritual truth is taught throughout the New Testament. God certainly has something to say to the seeking soul that He cannot impart to the person who ignores the truth and scorns the message in His Word. Spiritual truths cannot be received in the ordinary ways of human nature.

When the Revelation warns against this world, it is not so much a warning against the ways of this world as it is against the spirit of this world. This present world, in the New Testament meaning of the word, is simply unregenerate human nature no matter where it is found, even in the midst of zealous devotion to religion.

When Jesus came into our midst and presented Himself as the Messiah, His greatest enemies were the entrenched religious leaders of Israel. Their spiritual principles were drawn not from above, but from below. They used all the tactics of unregenerate men, including bribes, to bring the witness of lies against Jesus. To defend God, they acted like the devil. To claim support from the Scriptures, they defied its true teachings. In the name of a religion of love and mercy, they loosed the reins of blind hate. So fierce was their spirit—the spirit of this world that dominated them—that it never rested until they had put to death the Son of God.

Now, we are evangelicals at a troubled time in history. We face a danger—the danger of taking for granted that because we are evangelicals in theology and creed, we are automatically pleasing in the sight of God. Is it possible that our conservative theology is really a kind of nibbling of God's sweet and precious Word? Do we never allow it to become anything more than the creed and doctrines we say we believe?

The angel said to John, "Eat the scroll! Consume it! Digest it!" Jeremiah and Ezekiel testified that they ate and digested the Word of God, and then they went out to face bitterness and hostility. We are God's people for our day and our generation. God's people are called to be something different. God expects a certain kind of heroism from His redeemed people. Our call is not to a life of ease; we are called to be at our best for God and for His gospel.


## The sweetness of the Word stalls us

It appears at times that we are stalled by the sweetness of the Word of God. What a dear and treasured gift it is!

Maybe that is why we come to a halt. Maybe that is why we do not grow and mature in Christ as we should. We are being nurtured in the sweetness. We are prone, then, to refuse the discipline, to refuse the cross God lays upon us in the scoffing and ridicule of those who are still His enemies.

But Jesus is Victor! The faithful church in humility and submission will be exalted with Him, for ever and ever!

> And I saw a new heaven and a new earth: for the first heaven and the first earth were passed away; and there was no more sea . . . And I heard a great voice out of heaven saying, Behold, the tabernacle of God is with men, and he will dwell with them, and they shall be his people, and God himself shall be with them, and be their God . . .
>
> And he that sat upon the throne said, Behold, I make all things new. And he said unto me, Write: for these words are true and faithful . . .
>
> And I saw no temple therein: for the Lord God Almighty and the Lamb are the temple of it. And the city had no need of the sun, neither of the moon, to shine in it: for the glory of God did lighten it, and the Lamb is the light thereof. And the nations of them which are saved shall walk in the light of it: and the kings of the earth do bring their glory and honour into it. And the gates of it shall not be shut at all by day: for there shall be no night there. And they shall bring the glory and honour of the nations into it. And there shall in no wise enter into it any thing that defileth, neither whatsoever worketh abomination, or maketh a lie: but they which are written in the Lamb's book of life. (Revelation 21:1, 3, 5, 22-27)

On that day, the whole earth and all creation shall know it: Jesus Christ is Victor! Amen!

# TOZER

## GOD'S PURSUIT OF MAN

978-1-85078-051-9

# TOZER

## THE PRICE OF NEGLECT

978-1-85078-200-1

# TOZER

WE TRAVEL AN APPOINTED WAY

978-1-85078-116-5

# TOZER

## FAITH BEYOND REASON

978-1-85078-025-0